Resolution Family Disputes Handbook

Related titles from Law Society Publishing:

Child Law Handbook: Law and Practice
Liz Goldthorpe with Pat Munro

Civil Partnership: Law and Practice
Andrea Woelke

Domestic Abuse
Jane Wilson

Pensions and Family Breakdown (2nd edn)
David Davidson

Resolution Family Law Handbook (2nd edn)
General Editor: Andrew Greensmith

Tax and Family Breakdown
Jason Lane

Titles from Law Society Publishing can be ordered from all good bookshops or direct (telephone 0870 850 1422, email **lawsociety@prolog.uk.com** or visit our online shop at **www.lawsociety.org.uk/bookshop**).

RESOLUTION FAMILY DISPUTES HANDBOOK

General Editor: Andrew Greensmith

The Law Society

ISBN–13: 978-1-85328-714-5

Published in 2010 by the Law Society
113 Chancery Lane, London WC2A 1PL

Typeset by IDSUK (DataConnection) Ltd
Printed by TJ International Ltd, Padstow, Cornwall

FSC
Mixed Sources
Product group from well-managed forests and other controlled sources
Cert no. SGS-COC-2482
www.fsc.org
© 1996 Forest Stewardship Council

The paper used for the text pages of this book is FSC certified. FSC (the Forest Stewardship Council) is an international network to promote responsible management of the world's forests.

Contents

Foreword

One of the great changes that I have witnessed over the course of my professional life has been the arrival and steady development of alternative dispute resolution (ADR) as an alternative to litigation in family proceedings. From the original model of local mediation centres in odd corners run on shoestring budgets we now have a much more sophisticated concept of ADR, including early neutral evaluation, private judging, directive mediation, contracts for round-table discussions and collaborative law. Binding arbitration is a candidate for admission to provide the conflicted family with another alternative. Alongside this range lies the power and responsibility of the judge to conciliate within the framework of the contested proceedings.

While the courts do their best to respond to the ever-changing realities of family breakdown, they are often not the best place to solve parenting disputes, or prepare for the rebuilding of a damaged life after a relationship breakdown. So it is very exciting to see the Law Society widening the audience for Resolution's ADR work. The book is a practical rather than encyclopaedic work, which outlines modern alternatives to court and the advantages for all concerned.

The book repeatedly shows the three great benefits of ADR as opposed to the combative arena of the courts: ADR isolates problems, preserves an ongoing relationship and gives the parties ownership of the resolution process. There are no winners or losers.

At the same time, the book reveals the incredible commitment that ADR lawyers have put into developing, testing, perfecting and regulating new ways to help families through problems in the most constructive way, and exemplifies the thousands of hours put in to that end.

The book makes several timely interventions on current difficult issues facing ADR practitioners, including commenting on privilege, and the role of other professionals in these processes. It is a very valuable attempt by Resolution to pin down current best practice in a fast moving, international field.

Doubtless the landscape will continue to change apace; doubtless Resolution will continue to be one of its chief architects.

The Right Honourable Lord Justice Thorpe
Royal Courts of Justice
May 2010

About the editor and contributors

Tom Amlot is a partner and head of family practice at media firm Harbottle & Lewis LLP. His family work comprises all aspects of divorce including acting on high value ancillary relief matters, as well as private law cases involving children. Tom has a particular interest in the law of privacy in the context of family proceedings, as well as international aspects of family law. Tom is an accredited Resolution mediator and a collaborative lawyer.

Kim Beatson is head of the family law department at Anthony Gold, London Bridge. She specialises in all aspects of family law with an emphasis on finance, for both married and unmarried couples. Kim is an experienced mediator and a collaborative lawyer. She is a past chair of Resolution and is a Resolution accredited specialist in financial and cohabitation disputes.

Angela Donen is a partner at Bryan & Armstrong, Solicitors, in Mansfield, Nottinghamshire, specialising in finance and private children cases and mediation. She is a collaborative lawyer and has been an active mediator since 1996. She is a former vice chair of a hospital trust and is an accredited civil and commercial mediator. Angela is a member of the Family Mediators Association.

Joanne Edwards is a partner at Manches. She specialises in the whole range of issues which arise on the breakdown of a relationship and has extensive experience of cases with an international element. She has a particular interest in alternatives to court and was one of the first lawyers in this country to train as a collaborative lawyer, which is the mainstay of her practice. She is also a trained mediator. She sits on the national committee of Resolution and is vice chair of its alternative dispute resolution committee. She has featured widely in the media as a specialist commentator on family law issues. She speaks French and Spanish and is a lifelong Manchester United supporter.

Juliet Felton is a family consultant, psychotherapist/counsellor, family mediator and clinical supervisor. She works with couples or families before, during and after divorce to help them manage the emotional issues and difficulties of separation. Juliet is a member of the British Association for Counselling and Psychotherapy, the UK Association for Humanistic Psychology Practitioners and the Family Mediators' Association.

Kim Finnis runs her own niche family law practice in Guildford, Surrey, which she set up in 2002. She specialises in the financial aspects of divorce, and arrangements for children and is known for her constructive and sensible approach. She is an accredited Resolution mediator and a collaborative lawyer and also a Resolution accredited specialist. Kim is a past chair of Surrey Resolution and was a long-term committee member of that group. She is currently a member of Resolution's alternative dispute resolution committee.

Andrew Greensmith is head of private client and family law at Dickson Haslam. Andrew is a trained mediator, a practising collaborative lawyer, a member of the Chartered Institute of Arbitrators and is a deputy district judge. A former chair of Resolution, he now chairs their publications team. He is the editor of *Resolution Family Law Handbook*, second edition (Law Society 2010) and a co-author of *Claims under Schedule 1 to the Children Act 1989* (Resolution 2009).

Emma Harte has been a partner at Alexiou Fisher Philipps since 2001 and since qualification has been a member of Resolution. She is a fellow of the International Academy of Matrimonial Lawyers, a Resolution accredited mediator and trained collaborative lawyer and is chair of Resolution alternative dispute resolution committee and member of the International Academy of Collaborative Professionals. Emma is recommended in *Chambers Legal Directory* as a leading specialist family lawyer and recognised as 'a senior figure in the ADR Community'. The *Legal 500* also recognises her focus on mediation and collaborative law. Many of her cases involve an international element and involve complex financial issues. A number of her cases have been reported and she is a contributor to the *Resolution Family Law Handbook*, second edition (Law Society 2010).

William Hogg is a partner (manager) at Cambridge Family Law Practice specialising in complex financial matters. He is a mediator and a collaborative lawyer. He is a member of Resolution; the Family Mediators Association; the International Academy of Collaborative Professionals; Cambridge Collaborative Family Law Group (Treasurer); Resolution ADR committee, and the Union des Avocats Européens. William is a trainer with Resolution and a presenter of the foundation and skills courses for collaborative lawyers. He is recommended in both *Chambers Legal Directory* and the *Legal 500*.

Margaret Kelly is a partner in the family department at Seddons Solicitors, where she specialises in all aspects of family law. As a mediator and a collaborative lawyer, she explores the best option for each client. She is an accredited member of Resolution. Her specialist subjects are complex financial matters and private children issues. She has written articles for *The Review* and *Family Law*. She is a member of the Resolution alternative dispute resolution committee, Law Society family law panel, London collaborative law umbrella group and the International Academy of Collaborative Professionals.

Suzanne Kingston is head of family law at Dawsons LLP. She is widely known for her expertise in all aspects of family work, in particular the resolution of complex financial issues for high net worth individuals. Suzanne's cases often have an international element and she has considerable experience in dealing with prenuptial agreements and cohabitation issues. Suzanne has a thriving mediation practice and is a qualified collaborative lawyer and trains collaborative lawyers for Resolution. Suzanne lectures extensively and is often quoted in relation to family law matters.

Sarah Lloyd is Resolution's director of alternative dispute resolution (ADR). She is a former family lawyer, trained collaborative lawyer and accredited mediator. She now manages the ADR section of Resolution and promotes all forms of ADR in family matters in England and Wales.

James Pirrie with Rosemary Sands was instrumental in the arrival of collaborative law practice in the UK in 2003. He is an accredited mediator, having practised originally with the Institute of Family Therapy from the early 1990s and an active collaborative practitioner with particular interest in multidisciplinary work. He was the first European board member of the International Academy of Collaborative Professionals and is a long-serving member of Resolution's alternative dispute resolution committee.

Karen Ritchie runs a financial planning practice specialising in matters arising in divorce and separation. She is a Resolution accredited independent financial adviser. She contributes regularly to publications aimed at increasing the financial awareness of those going through divorce. Most recently she helped edit the Money Made Clear website on divorce and separation.

Neil Robinson is director of The Mediation Centre at Nowell Meller Solicitors, Stafford. He was Legal Aid Family Lawyer of the Year 2007. He is a trainer for the Family Mediators' Association and Resolution, an experienced family lawyer, family and civil mediator and professional practice consultant, and a mental health tribunal judge. He has a particular enthusiasm for developing creative mediation practice that will meet the needs of entrenched, hybrid and complex cases, and has written about this extensively in *Family Law 2008–9* (Jordans). His ageing world music band, *Fish from Oblivion*, is engaged on a world tour of the surviving Staffordshire pubs.

Jonathan Southgate is a barrister at 29 Bedford Row Chambers and was called to the Bar in 1992. His main area of practice is high net worth ancillary relief. He has been instructed on a number of very media-sensitive cases and also advises on complex prenuptial agreements. He regularly writes and lectures on a range of subjects, is a member of the Family Law Bar Association, an affiliate member of Resolution, and is ranked as a leading junior in all of the relevant publications.

Table of cases

Table of legislation

STATUTES

STATUTORY INSTRUMENTS

EUROPEAN

A note on terminology

The term most usually adopted in this jurisdiction to describe out-of-court resolution processes is 'alternative dispute resolution' (ADR).

Many practitioners working in this area feel that this is an inappropriate term to describe these processes, which they think should be considered before any court process is initiated. In an effort to describe these processes more accurately, a number of terms have been suggested by practitioners, such as '*appropriate* dispute resolution', '*constructive* dispute resolution' and '*other* dispute resolution'. Some of these terms appear in this book.

In Australia, the term '*primary* dispute resolution' has been formally adopted to describe all forms of non-court dispute resolution methods, relegating the last resort option, the court, to the alternative or secondary role. The authors of this book all hope that a similar approach will be adopted soon in this jurisdiction.

CHAPTER 1

Unresolved conflict

Emma Harte

1.1 WHAT IS CONFLICT?

'Conflict' is defined in the Collins *English Dictionary* as being 'a struggle', 'trial of strength', 'disagreement'.

Most couples will conflict with each other from time to time; that is natural and all part of being in a healthy relationship. There are few couples who agree on everything all of the time.

Most couples go through bad patches when arguing seems to be their only activity. Many couples survive these rough patches and succeed in resolving their issues. However, problems arise with those who do not resolve their issues.

1.2 CONFLICT IN FAMILIES

People who have grown up in an argumentative family often find themselves within argumentative relationships and marriages. That is their way and they may not be displaying real anger. Some people, however, dislike confrontation and try to avoid arguments wherever possible.

Where there are issues that are not voiced and remain unresolved, there are bound to be problems. A counsellor can assist with helping couples to work out the problems but if problems fester, a home can become a battleground rather than a haven of peace and tranquillity from the outside world.

Splitting up or divorce sometimes is the next step but it should only be considered when the relationship or marriage has finally and irretrievably broken down.

Not many children of separating or divorcing parents welcome a break up. Many children would much rather have their parents living together even if the atmosphere in the family is difficult and tense. However, it is well known that much of the damage inflicted on children of separating and divorcing parents occurs in the period before the decision to split up is taken and before the children have been told that their parents are intending to separate or divorce. Children who have witnessed violence between their parents are even more likely to be traumatised.

During this period, parents are likely to be stressed, angry, depressed and tired and, consequently, each may put more pressure than normal on the other. For example, where either parent usually would be happy to take their child to an activity, neither now has the energy to do so and each wants the other to do it. The child can only guess from this that neither parent wants to be with him or her. Alternatively, one or both parents may become more closely involved with the child and possibly more possessive. That too becomes a pressure which the child picks up on.

Children can feel that the deterioration of family life is their fault and worry that their parents will no longer be around for them. The more this is felt, the more they are likely to withdraw into themselves or to become very clingy and tearful.

Research in the UK and elsewhere has shown clearly that children are often miserable and insecure when they are subjected to constant parental arguments. The ways in which parental quarrels upset children are not always easy to understand. It was clear, however, from *The Exeter Family Study* (1994) carried out by Monica Cockett and Dr John Tripp that from the children's point of view, certain levels and kinds of disagreements were more upsetting than others. Children's behaviour and educational achievement are also affected by parental conflict long before separation or divorce.

1.3 THE CHILD PSYCHIATRIST'S VIEW

Dr Mark Berelowitz FRCPsych, Consultant Child and Adolescent Psychiatrist at the Royal Free Hospital, Hampstead, London spoke of the factors that affect children's psychological well-being during and following divorce in a talk that he gave at the launch of the London family collaborative lawyers in November 2006. He said:

1. Children do best if they have full and rich relationships with both parents. This means homework, discipline and vegging out, as well as fun.
2. Discord between parents, in marriage and divorce, is the most powerful environmental factor which impacts on children's psychological well-being.
3. The quality of the relationship between the parents predicts the quality and quantity of contact between the children and the non-resident parent. Children are capable of forming close relationships with step parents without damaging the relationship with the parent of that gender.

Dr Berelowitz spoke about the fact that the standard legal approach had considerable potential to encourage bad behaviour, i.e. behaviour which increases discord. On the whole, in his view, it discouraged compromise and he explained how it was hard for someone in his position to work with a couple who had exchanged 'profoundly critical and denigrating' witness statements. It was for that reason that he hoped more couples would turn to the collaborative process and other forms of dispute resolution, as although an authoritative decision from on high could sometimes be required, more often than not such decisions and the process to get to those decisions were not conducive to harmonious post-divorce or post-hearing relationships.

He also pointed out that all children told him that they preferred an outcome which both parents perceived to be fair and queried how often both parents came away from contested proceedings with a mutually agreed sense of a fair outcome as opposed to resolving matters out of court.

1.4 GOOD PARENTING AND RESOLUTION'S COMMITMENT TO PARENTING AFTER PARTING

Each year, some 30,000 children in the UK experience the separation of their parents. Overall, more than one in three children will see their parents split up before they reach their sixteenth birthday.

Resolution lawyers are committed to helping parents to manage their separation in the best interests of their children. We believe that having access early on in the process to good information and resources is a key factor in how well parents and their children will be able to cope with the separation. To this end, Resolution has produced a booklet designed to give parents critical important information at an early stage, *Divorce and Separation: Choosing the Right Process for You* (2009). The material set out in the booklet covers a range of topics about the separation process as well as information about how children are affected at different ages and can be helped.

CHAPTER 2

Principles and values

James Pirrie

2.1 THE ROLE OF RESOLUTION

Resolving disputes through dialogue was a core commitment of the 1981 founders of the organisation that was to become Resolution. They expressed a commitment to what was then called conciliation. So it is little wonder that Resolution has been so strong a presence in the development of these practices.

2.2 WHAT ARE RESOLUTION PROFESSIONALS HERE TO DO?

Since that time and particularly following 1997, when Resolution became a mediation training organisation and 2004 when it adopted the new collaborative organisation, matters have moved significantly. Alternatives are a core element for Resolution professionals – or rather court is increasingly where it should be: the last resort. That is because what we believe in is informed, client-directed, child-oriented resolution – and that can be better secured through assisted dialogue.

The extent of the stresses of relationship breakdown and the complexity of the issues arising from that breakdown mean that few couples will manage the whole process well on their own. Most will find their way to better decisions through the support of a professional, helping them to tease out their options and assess the routes and approaches that will best suit their circumstances and guide them through the steps required by those choices.

So we grieve over the relentless cutbacks to public funding, excluding many from the support from which they would benefit and which would benefit their children, which only results, for so many families, in problems becoming cases (at even greater cost to the public purse). Professionals however should work hard to fill the gap, so far as can be done, e.g. by operating efficiently, so as to lower costs and make these services as widely available up and down the economic scale as possible.

2.3 THE LIMITATIONS OF COURT-BASED OUTCOMES

Too often, court-style approaches are:

- standardised, speaking to the preferences and norms of the professionals rather than the clients who must live with the outcome;
- reached only after an overly costly and delayed process.

They satisfy no one (we have all heard the judges say in quiet moments that often their aspiration is to impose an outcome equally disappointing to all parties) and ignore elements that may have been of crucial importance to the clients.

Many of the matters that are of greatest importance to clients, the court is simply unable to manage or deliver effectively – this is particularly the case given that so many solutions are found only at the end and the period beforehand can seem an unregulated wilderness where whatever goes. Interim maintenance solutions are only available after delays – and often at prohibitive cost – but the needs are immediate. Building good transitions for children at the outset, when parents are separating, would have crucial benefits for the entire family but the court cannot regulate such arrangements.

Often the outcomes themselves are the sort that might have been envisaged right at the outset and indeed often-times secured before all the costs were encountered by the family, if only there had been the willingness to step into the right settlement zone. So a court-style solution may be seen as a limiting sort of target for clients looking to resolve their issues.

2.4 THE NEED FOR COURT-BASED SOLUTIONS FOR SOME

The courts offer an externally imposed outcome that does not depend on the willingness of parties to reach agreement. The court process is necessary; without it, there is no need to negotiate – strength will prevail. The kinds of constructive dispute resolution we are looking at in this book do not exist without the court structure and the better the court structure runs, the better must be our dispute resolution processes. For a minority, a court-directed outcome is necessary, perhaps as a result of the characters or the issues arising from the dispute that involves them. However, beyond this relatively narrow group, there is a broad range of people who will not find their best solutions arising from preparations for a court hearing, with all the resource outlay that this involves. (One bears in mind how few of these cases eventually reach a solution imposed by judicial decision.)

This majority is likely to benefit from a process that offers:

- greater involvement for them;
- the possibility of better solutions, through engaging their creativity; and

- greater likelihood of more child-focused outcomes because of giving greater voice to the clients' knowledge of their family's situation and through building better longer-term communication patterns between parents.

2.5 THE ESSENTIALS OF ALTERNATIVE DISPUTE RESOLUTION (ADR)

It is difficult to find a definition or description of alternative dispute resolution (ADR) in family issues that works for all purposes, all professionals and no matter what jurisdiction. The essential success-potential of dispute resolution methods shifts between types, depending on the intentions of the clients and, no doubt, the experience of the professional. We suggest that common to better performing resolution processes will be:

- a focus upon the positive;
- the building of stronger, longer-term relationships between the clients (particularly where they are then stronger to benefit the children);
- the building of outcomes that focus on what matters to the clients rather than just the issues that would be recognised in a dispute brought before a court; and
- the issues, solutions and outcome modelled largely, or – more usually – entirely by the clients of the family law professionals, the latter being engaged by the clients to map out and operate the process by which these issues are identified, the solutions examined and the outcomes achieved.

2.6 THE POTENTIAL OF ADR

ADR is a broad church: not only does it contain many processes, it also encompasses many different sorts of intent. At one end, it may be pursued by clients or professionals as a means of securing broadly court-like outcomes but at lower cost and without the trauma that the court process is seen as risking. At the other end are those who are able to achieve beneficial transformation through rising to the challenges that their separations create.

What they have in common is an awareness of the limitations of court-style approaches. That said, seeking a 'court-like outcome, but cheaper and a bit nicer' would be viewed by experienced ADR professionals as a fairly low aspiration. When we are working at our best:

- We are starting to find and address the core or underlying conflict between the parties.
- We are creating, in the parties, the growing realisation of the possibility of a better future.
- We may be helping the parties to find better means of communication which will improve their longer-term relationship.

- We are starting to engage the parties' creativity in the outcome.
- We may be working towards solutions that could never have been on the menu at court.
- We are certainly doing our work with an appreciation of where our clients are stationed in the grief and recovery curve and ideally working with them in a way that helps to progress that journey from divorced or separated to independent.

2.7 FROM POSITIONS TO INTERESTS

Position-based negotiation lies so much at the core of our court-based process that, at an early stage, we have stopped even noticing its influence – let alone questioning whether it provides the best way forward. In financial matters, Form E requires us to set out the form of the order we seek; financial dispute resolution (FDR) hearings start with a request for clarity as regards the offers made by each side and progress usually with a series of offers and counter-offers; final hearings require the filing of position statements. In private children work it is the same, with positions being set out from the issue of proceedings onwards.

Central to the way in which dispute resolution is now practised is the focus on interests: positions are avoided and any demand set down by one side is used more as a stepping stone to understand that client's interests and needs. Once we understand the needs that lie on each side then we are in a position to engage the creativity of the participants to work out a wider range of options that might better meet more of the clients' interests and needs.

And when we focus on needs and interests, generally we move away from the conflict (the natural reaction when we are confronted by someone's stated position) and we may start to engage a slowly developing empathy within the room as each side learns more about the deeper concerns of the other.

As soon as there is empathy, then there is the start of a willingness to find solutions that work for all those affected by the dispute and these are likely to be the building blocks of better solutions.

2.8 CLIENT BUY-IN AND ASPIRATIONS: THE CORNERSTONES OF SUCCESSFUL ADR

What lies at the core of this higher-level work are two core building blocks. All too often our dispute resolution processes fail because whilst we have successfully avoided putting ourselves – as the professionals – at the centre of the outcome and resisted relying on the court, we have, nonetheless, failed to help our clients take control of their future for themselves. What is really needed first is to help clients clarify their aspirations and identify what matters to them, and secondly to obtain buy-in: as the professional, we must obtain our clients' permission to hold them to those aspirations as the principles that will guide our progress.

Without these core components, our process is on thin ice. However, if we have managed these two steps well then we have foundations strong enough to address even profoundly difficult conflicts.

We will come to the role of aspirations after looking at buy-in.

2.8.1 Buy-in

Buy-in comes from fully informed consent. Where the professional has laid out the options fully and tried to give the client a real sense of the up and downsides of each of them, then the process selected was the free choice of the client, who also takes responsibility for its working. Conversely, where the professional advocates a particular selection then the choice is the professional's and she or he is responsible for the success of the process. The client can sit back and watch it perform without responsibility.

As long as the process is the client's choice and the professional is clear about the ground rules then the client has committed to working within the system. So professionals will want to ensure that the client is informed about the structures and principles of the process at the outset and does not feel ambushed by them when they are called into play.

That is why the proper ADR practitioner is often also a committed litigator in his or her spare time. It is the practitioner's knowledge of each of the realistic options that enables the client to trust him or her as a guide – it is because of the relative lack of professional interest over the choice (as would exist if the only services the professional offered were litigation or collaboration) that the client can believe that she or he is getting a disinterested view of the options. It is because the practitioner can take the client through what litigation would really be like and what it would produce, and compare and contrast that against the ADR options, that the client is able to make an informed choice. The professional who offers each of the services can have a real advantage in gaining the client's trust at the time of process selection.

2.8.2 Aspirations of the clients

The harder the case, the longer you are likely to want to spend on aspirations. Clients, even those appearing in deep conflict, tend to have highly convergent aspirations – or where they do not they are likely to be highly accepting or even approving of each other's aspirations. Finding this common ground amid apparent conflict provides strong foundations for a resolution.

The more the aspirations are mapped out and detailed, the more that the clients buy into them as offering the touchstone that will inform what is acceptable and what is not, what is productive and what is not.

It may be hard for clients to understand what is needed to speak about aspirations without laying out positions. We have often got them on the right track by talking about the two elements:

- **Substance:** what (looking forwards, when you have reached the agreement) do you want this outcome to enable all of you as family members to be able to do?
- **Process:** what (looking backwards, after having reached the agreement) do you want to be able to say about how you did it?

The aspirations as to substance tell us what we are working towards and the aspirations as to process give us the ground rules for how we are going to work on the problems in the room.

2.9 CORE VALUES

So we can start to identify some of the key themes that are respected within the ADR community – as the values that (a) inform how we work as professionals, and (b) help us to work successfully for our clients (see **Table 2.1**).

2.9.1 An audit to identify the better option for the client

In *Getting Ready to Negotiate* (Penguin Group USA, 1995), Roger Fisher and Danny Ertel recommended that the following questions be raised by professionals in considering whether a particular resolution process was one likely to be valuable to the client:

1. Interests: will the process help each side to understand what the other wants?
2. Options: will it generate a wide range of possible solutions?
3. Alternatives: will it make the clients aware of what their alternative is if they walk away from this process?
4. Legitimacy: will it help clients to know whether what they are proposing is fair and appropriate?
5. Communication: will it improve communication?
6. Relationship: will it build the relationship for the future?
7. Commitment: will it result in a deal that can be relied upon?

An additional set of criteria might be the following:

8. Will the client feel supported?
9. Will the process be effective to deliver a shared understanding of what is at issue (including full disclosure where relevant)?
10. Will it achieve conclusion?
11. Is it cost-effective?

Table 2.1 The ADR philosphy

Values relating to the development of our profession	Values relating to our work for clients
Access to justice/the importance of clients having access to professional support and the courts where needed. Mindset of plenty – we believe that others succeeding within the ADR community are likely to help our own practice; and what follows from this is: • a belief in sharing what we have and have learned with each other; • respect for other disciplines and other models – we look to engage with other professionals who will assist our clients in their journey.	Hearing and addressing the story of the client – we aim to grasp the complaint rooted in the history of their relationship. Clients identify the issues: if it matters to the clients then we should find a way of addressing these matters rather than just the ones that seem usual for the professional. Informed client decision making – only when the client understands, can s/he buy into the process choices we offer, adopt the ground rules that are necessary for progress and make an informed choice on a particular set of outcomes. Long-term perspectives: the choices that the client makes should stand the test of time because they are: • child focused; • relationship affirming; • peace-building; • interest-based bargaining rather than positional bargaining; • positive client aspirations providing the guidelines for progress rather than vague predictions of likely court outcome.

12. Is it paced appropriately for the participants?
13. Is it effective at neutralising or managing power imbalance between the parties?
14. Does it offer opportunities for the clients to be creative and are the outcomes self-determined?
15. What is the risk of regret in the longer term?

When we have identified the key concerns of the clients then we are in a position to start to audit their process choices and help them assess which of them will best meet their needs. If the route will engage their higher and longer-term interests then they will truly have started on a path of informed, client-directed, child-oriented decision making.

CHAPTER 3

Options

Joanne Edwards

The word 'options' signifies the availability of a range of possible paths which give power or freedom to individuals to choose their own destiny. Even when going through a traumatic life experience such as divorce or separation, it is important that an individual should be afforded this level of autonomy.

As practitioners, our values require us to facilitate an honest and authentic engagement with a client's needs. It is an important part of the role we play that we help individuals and families to identify their options; to understand the workings of each such option; and to select the best option, having applied appropriate criteria. This can be done through a verbal description of the various processes, as well as by reference to written tools such as Resolution's booklet *Divorce and Separation: Choosing the Right Process for You* (2009).

This chapter will look at the different options available to clients, assessing them by reference to the different priorities and values that each client may have. Later chapters will look at the individual processes in more detail.

3.1 WHAT ARE THE CLIENT'S OPTIONS WHEN SHE OR HE FIRST CONSULTS A FAMILY LAWYER?

At a first meeting with a family lawyer, the client faces a vast (and sometimes intimidating) range of options.

Among the most basic options with which a new client is confronted are: should I instigate a divorce or separation now, or are there reconciliation options which I have yet to attempt or exhaust? Should I pursue matters now or at a later date? If there is to be a divorce, who is going to issue the petition and on what fact? How 'hands on' do I want my lawyer to be in any financial negotiations with my spouse? What are the qualities I am looking for in my lawyer? Do I sense the correct *fit* with the lawyer in front of me, or should I instruct another? (Of course, this particular decision will involve various factors, including analyses of competing charge-out rates/reputations/style of lawyer.)

Once that raft of basic options has been considered and decisions made, a whole substratum of process options opens up. These process options relate to how the client or family in question is going to resolve the issues surrounding the breakdown of the relationship.

There is a range of such options open to separating and divorcing couples. Each family is different and individual circumstances, priorities and values will determine which method is favoured in that case. What is most important is that separating and divorcing couples need to be fully informed of all available process options at the outset, and at appropriate stages throughout their case, so that they can make an informed decision about how best to resolve their dispute.

The main process options available to couples upon divorce or separation are as follows.

3.1.1 To negotiate their own agreement

Many clients, especially in more challenging economic times, endeavour to work out as much of the detail of an agreement as possible before consulting lawyers. This will not be suitable for everyone (e.g. where there is inequality of bargaining power or imbalance of knowledge about the finances or unrealistic expectations on the part of one or both of the parties); and couples may still need some legal advice in order to ensure they know their rights and understand the full implications of any agreements and decisions they make.

3.1.2 Traditional negotiation through solicitors

This is the most commonly used method. Negotiation can take place at any stage, with or without court proceedings in the background, and can take the form of written proposals or round-table settlement meetings (or a combination of both).

The Resolution round-table protocol grew out of a workshop given in London in 2004, where concern was expressed that professionals were launching into meetings with no discussion of the nuts and bolts of duration, how they would be conducted, their purpose, or even what status would be given to the information shared within them. It was felt that there was a need for a set of ground rules on how such meetings might be run.

The protocol was Resolution's endeavour to provide these rules. They provide a safer way to conduct meetings which, when set against the ethical commitments that exist in the collaborative process, are relatively unsafe.

The form of the agreement can be downloaded from the members' section of the Resolution website (**www.resolution.org.uk**) and is not intended to be fixed – practitioners are likely to want to import other principles – but it is intended to provide at least a minimal level of safety.

3.1.3 Mediation

Mediation is a way of resolving disputes and difficult issues between separating couples. It has a long history. The main characteristics are:

- Mediators can help with all the issues faced by separating couples, or to resolve specific issues such as arrangements for any children. They can do so as an adjunct to court proceedings, or without any proceedings having been issued.
- Mediators are trained to help people resolve disputes. A mediator will meet with the couple together, usually three to five times, and will help to identify issues in dispute and help to try and reach agreement themselves.
- Mediators are neutral and will not take sides. They are not advisers and cannot give legal advice. They will usually recommend that each party obtains separate legal advice alongside the mediation process.
- Mediation can help couples to retain control over their future, enter into constructive negotiations and to come to flexible or unique solutions tailor-made for their families.
- At the conclusion of the mediation the mediator will prepare a summary of the mutually acceptable proposals together with a summary of the financial information which will be sent to each party to discuss with their lawyers. After receiving legal advice where appropriate, the lawyers will convert the summary into a legally binding document and carry out any necessary implementation.

3.1.4 Collaborative law

The collaborative law process arrived in England and Wales in 2003. Its fundamental planks are that:

- Each person appoints their own (collaboratively trained) lawyer, but rather than negotiations being conducted by letter or phone, the clients and the lawyers all get together at a series of meetings to work things out face to face. Therefore each client has their lawyer's support and legal advice as the matter progresses.
- Collaborative lawyers sign an agreement with the clients (the participation agreement) that disqualifies them from representing the client in court if the collaborative process breaks down. This is arguably the key to the success of the process as it means that everyone is absolutely committed to finding the best solutions by agreement, rather than through conflict.
- Where appropriate, other professionals can be brought into the collaborative process to assist the couple with issues relating to the finances (such as independent financial advisers (IFAs), actuaries, valuers) or relationship or children issues (therapists or family counsellors). Sometimes these other professionals will work with the couple in the meetings with the lawyers, or they will meet separately with the couple or one party.
- Collaborative law can be used to resolve any issues arising from relationship breakdown. It can be a particularly appealing process when children

are involved and there is a need to maintain good relations, including ongoing communications about the children and their welfare.

- The clients set the agenda. Clients find that the collaborative approach helps reduce stress by allowing them to do things at their own pace and remain in control of a process which is often seen as alien and intimidating.
- Once an agreement is reached, the lawyers can put it into effect. The divorce can be finalised and a consent order sent to the court for approval.

3.1.5 Cooperative law

A controversial recent addition, but one which cannot be ignored, is cooperative law (also known as 'collab-lite'). The process mirrors the collaborative process, save that the participation agreement does not include the disqualification clause that precludes the parties from issuing proceedings through their collaborative lawyers. Many would say that this runs directly contrary to the fundamental spirit of collaborative law; its advocates argue that it allows clients to try to resolve matters amicably but without the costs and other consequences if the process breaks down.

3.1.6 Arbitration

As decisions in family matters reached through arbitration are not binding in England and Wales, this is not currently a very popular option. Arbitration entails the couple and their lawyers agreeing on a suitably qualified arbitrator to hear their case and give a decision. This gives couples a choice of decision maker, continuity, privacy and confidentiality, flexibility of hearing dates and venue and avoidance of court delay. A downside is the expense, as – unlike in a court hearing – the venue and the arbitrator must be paid for by the couple. For high profile well-off couples the benefits of a private hearing and a final decision that would remain unreported in the media would likely outweigh this consideration. In the wake of the rules surrounding transparency, which came into force in 2009, this option may increase in popularity.

3.1.7 Litigation

A judicially imposed outcome may be the final option once other methods have been exhausted, or in cases where there are intractable disputes or personalities not suitable to alternative dispute resolution (ADR). The imperfections associated with the court process are well rehearsed (delay; usually irreparable damage to a couple's relationship, of particular concern where there are young children; outcomes with which one party will invariably be unhappy and therefore reluctant to honour; and generally, the difficulties associated with asking a judge with a heavy workload to make a decision about a family about which they know relatively little). Such imperfections have led to calls for couples to be required to attempt ADR in certain instances before they are permitted to issue court proceedings, e.g. in children cases.

3.2 COLLABORATIVE LAW AND MEDIATION COMPARED

The processes are similar in various ways:

- Both processes assist separating couples in reaching a tailored outcome that takes into account their particular circumstances.
- Both aim to assist couples in resolving issues without recourse to the court.
- Both rely on face-to-face negotiation in the form of a number of meetings.
- Both give control over the decision-making process and the pace at which it proceeds to the separating couple.
- Both enable the parties to keep details of their discussions, and of the outcome reached, confidential and away from the glare of publicity.
- Both help to enable the couple to maintain civil relations after the process is over.
- Both can be used to resolve the full range of issues associated with a separation: the dissolution of the relationship, arrangements for the children, reaching agreement about the finances, etc.

The key differences are:

- In mediation, one person facilitates the discussions in a series of meetings between the separating couple. In the collaborative process both parties have their lawyers present throughout the meetings (although lawyers can be present in mediation if it is felt appropriate).
- A mediator cannot give legal advice or assist either party in presenting their position to the other as it is central to that process that she or he must remain unbiased at all times. The collaborative process provides each party with immediate access to advice on proposed options as the discussions develop.
- In mediation legal advice must be given outside the process by the parties' respective legal advisers. In the collaborative process legal advice is usually given within the process and to both of the parties jointly. Giving advice to one's own client outside the four-way meetings is undesirable and to the extent that has happened, the lawyers will be encouraged to divulge in the four-way meeting any advice they have given.
- In collaborative law the job of the lawyers is to assist their individual clients to remain focused and positive at all times. Each person is supported in the negotiations. Clients can have separate meetings with their own lawyer but all negotiations take place in four-way meetings with both

parties and both lawyers present. In mediation a client has to maintain focus for him or herself.

- Mediators cannot draw up legally binding agreements. Each party must instruct a lawyer to obtain separate independent legal advice during and at the end of the mediation process. The lawyers instructed will consider the final document prepared by the mediator (the memorandum of understanding), advise the client on its terms, convert this document into a legally binding one and then file all appropriate documents at court on behalf of the parties.
- Collaborative practitioners can deal with all issues on behalf of their clients including drafting the appropriate documents once the negotiations are complete. If negotiations do break down and the parties decide to go to court then the collaborative practitioners are contractually bound to cease acting and new lawyers must be instructed.

3.3 WHAT IS THE IMPORTANCE TO THE CLIENT OF OPTIONS?

In any setting, the most obvious benefit of having a range of options is that the route chosen can be determined by reference to the individual's own needs and priorities. Nowhere is that more so than in relation to family breakdown, where all sorts of emotions and motivations are at play. These considerations will mean that great care is needed in selecting a process option at the beginning.

Quite apart from trying to determine the correct process option at the outset, it is important to review regularly that initial decision. Depending upon how a case develops, it may be that other options need to be explored along the way. For example, a mediator can be brought into the collaborative process if waters become choppy; cost or other considerations may mean that clients decide to engage in some direct discussions themselves; or issues which looked resolvable may have become intractable, needing judicial input.

All of this reinforces the need for a wide range of process options in family cases. Against this backdrop, therefore, it is important for a family lawyer to undertake an audit at the initial client meeting, and regularly thereafter, in order to determine what are the characteristics and priorities of the individual client or family; and therefore which process option they are most likely to favour.

The sort of questions which a family lawyer should reflect upon when advising upon process options will likely include the following.

3.3.1 What stage in the grief curve have the client and his spouse reached?

In many cases, one party ('the *leaver*') will have long since reached the decision to bring the relationship to an end, whilst the other ('the *leavee*') will still be reeling from the shock of only recently having learned of this state of affairs. The leaver may be in a new relationship, or may have decided for other reasons that he wishes to proceed quickly with a divorce. The leavee will be confronted with a range of painful emotions and will not be able to make decisions quickly or rationally. The ability to dictate the pace of non-court-based processes will appeal to the leavee, as she will be afforded more time to deal with her emotions and will then be better placed to engage in settlement discussions. However there is always a risk that the leaver will become disillusioned by his inability to force the pace and there may come a point when he craves the certainty of having a court-imposed timetable.

3.3.2 How quickly does the client wish to reach a conclusion?

This follows on from the previous question. It may be that one is in the fortunate position of having two spouses who are at the same stage of the grief curve. However, one of them may still have reasons for wishing to progress more slowly than the other may desire. An obvious example is where one spouse has been made redundant during or just before proceedings. That spouse may decide tactically to rush negotiations, to get maintenance pegged by reference to the new circumstances; whilst the other spouse may prefer to slow things right down and wait for the first spouse to secure new employment before negotiating (which would also avoid the need to revisit maintenance at a later date).

3.3.3 What is the state of the client's knowledge about the family's finances?

If one's client demonstrates little or no knowledge of their family's finances at the initial meeting, some may shy away from advocating ADR processes. There is a perception that mediation (and collaborative law) can provide a good forum for the non-discloser. However, the mere fact of one party having limited knowledge does not mean that one cannot rely on the other spouse to provide full and frank disclosure, even in mediation or the collaborative process. In reality, this question should be considered in conjunction with the next.

3.3.4 What is the extent of any dialogue between the couple to date in the context of a separation or divorce and how amicably has that dialogue progressed?

Proper buy-in and cooperation from both parties is key to any non-court-based process option. As such it is essential to obtain from one's client a sense of what discussions surrounding divorce or separation have taken place with the other spouse so far and what progress was made. It is also key to look for non-verbal signs. The vast majority of clients who see a lawyer for the first time will say that they and their spouse aspire to an amicable divorce and, where applicable, wish to preserve their relationship for the benefit of the children. However, where those sentiments are coupled with the other spouse having e.g. substantially restricted one's client's access to income on an interim basis, or emptied the bank accounts, one obviously has to question seriously their commitment to resolving matters amicably.

3.3.5 Is there equality of bargaining power between the parties?

Although a skilled mediator will be able to rectify any imbalance of bargaining power between spouses, many clients shy away from this process option if they are genuinely anxious at the prospect of direct negotiation with their spouse in the presence of a person who is there to facilitate discussion rather than argue one party's corner. Such clients will also be reluctant to engage in direct discussions with their spouse. Conversely, all of the other process options will entail each client having a lawyer beside them along the way to provide advice and support.

3.3.6 Has there been or is there ongoing domestic abuse?

It can be easy to forget that domestic abuse can affect families from any walk of life, and can affect men as well as women. Many clients feel shame and will not readily volunteer that they have been victims; it can take extensive and sensitive questioning to get to the truth. Having done this, the lawyer needs to make an assessment of the risk which presently exists. If protection is required, the court process will need to be instigated. If the risk is properly adjudged to have passed, alternatives to court may still prove to be viable (and indeed better for the parties than the court process).

3.3.7 How realistic are the client's settlement aspirations?

It is important to have regard to the client's stated settlement aims and whether they are within the bounds of what a court would order. For example, a client who says that he will pay no (or limited) maintenance to his soon to be ex-wife, despite the fact that she has not worked outside the home for 10 years and is raising young children, is unlikely to be well advised to proceed down the collaborative route, and is not likely to get far in traditional or direct negotiations. He may benefit from mediation, with a skilled mediator reality-checking his proposals with his wife present; or he may need direction from a judge or an arbitrator.

3.3.8 How receptive is the client to advice?

In conjunction with the previous question, one must gauge how likely one's client is to depart from unrealistic aspirations with the benefit of legal advice.

A client may well be unrealistic at first but change his views once he has been given advice by reference to statute and case law. However, the client who is not receptive to legal advice is not going to be appreciative of his lawyer going into the collaborative setting and agreeing with his collaborative colleague that the correct parameters of settlement are precisely those which the client has rejected.

3.3.9 How involved in the process does the client want to be?

This is an important consideration. Many clients are keen to proceed through the mediation or collaborative routes precisely because of the high level of involvement they have in the process. Quite apart from being able to control the pace and direction which the discussions take, they find it empowering to be able to have their say and determine their own destiny. For others this is an uncomfortable place to be. They would far sooner have a lawyer as a mouthpiece and be involved only to the extent of giving instructions on points as they arise, without being more directive.

3.3.10 How complex and unprecedented are the issues?

Whilst the fact of substantial assets alone will not militate against non-court-based options, the existence of difficult issues may. If there are issues in respect of which there is no guidance in reported cases, it may be difficult to resolve those issues without court input. It may be a case of keeping the process options under review, starting with an ADR process but then bringing the matter in front of a judge or an arbitrator if no resolution can be found.

3.4 APPLYING THE INFORMATION ACQUIRED TO THE OPTIONS AVAILABLE

Having obtained answers to the questions set out in the previous section, the family lawyer is likely to have formed a better idea about the suitability of the individual client or family to particular process options and likely incompatibility with other options.

In relation to collaborative law, the experience acquired to date suggests that most cases ought to be capable of progressing through this process option. For example, although the majority of collaborative cases undertaken so far in this jurisdiction have involved relatively modest levels of assets, there have been cases which have proceeded (successfully) through the collaborative law route where the assets run to tens of millions of pounds. Cases with apparently complex facts and issues in dispute have also been resolved through this route.

Collaborative law may be felt to be inappropriate, and litigation or arbitration more apt, where there are suspicions about one spouse not being full and frank in his financial disclosure; where there are issues as to the appropriate jurisdiction for any divorce and fears that to seek to 'talk first, issue later' could lead to a negligence claim if the other spouse then rushes off to issue in another jurisdiction, especially in Europe; if one party has very little knowledge of the financial landscape in the case (although of course collaborative law would not be precluded in those circumstances if that spouse is comfortable that the other will cooperate in the disclosure process); if there have been any signs that one party has unrealistic views and aspirations about the parameters of settlement and is unlikely to change his position; or if there is a discrepancy of opinion about the speed with which any discussions should ensue.

Of course, the comforts that clients derive from the collaborative process are that it is transparent; all legal advice is given within the four-way setting; the clients themselves are able to participate fully, whilst having the comfort of knowing that the lawyers will also be present; the parties are not positional in their bargaining, but truly seek to agree what they perceive to be the bracket of settlement and work from there; and neither party can rush off and issue court proceedings at a moment's notice.

When deciding whether mediation is an appropriate process option in a given case, slightly different considerations apply. Clients engaging in mediation have the option of formally instructing solicitors and issuing court proceedings without the time and cost implications that collaborative clients will face, so there are not the same concerns about whether each spouse will give full and frank disclosure, whether there may prove to be insurmountable complexities or issues between the parties, etc. A skilled mediator can deal with most potential pitfalls, including imbalance of bargaining power between the parties, complex facts and the resulting detailed financial disclosure, triangulation, etc.

Of course, the main advantage to clients of progressing through mediation is that they will feel a great sense of achievement if they manage to broker an agreement. Because the mediator is not likely to be directive, the parties will rightly engage in some self-congratulation if they do reach agreement. The clients also have the protection of knowing that no binding agreement will be reached in mediation, as the drawing up of a memorandum of understanding will then provide them with the opportunity to take legal advice.

3.5 HOW DIRECTIVE SHOULD ONE BE WHEN GOING THROUGH A CLIENT'S OPTIONS?

A difficult question, and one in respect of which there are varying opinions, is the extent to which one should guide a client down a particular process option route once we have given them details of all of the process options.

As family lawyers, it is our instinct to guide clients in respect of every aspect of their case. There is a temptation, particularly where we sense that a client is feeling vulnerable, to present solutions rather than options. It could also be said, with some justification, that clients who are faced with this smorgasbord of options at the outset are not in the best place emotionally to make the correct decision. Many feel strongly that they are paying a lawyer for advice and they want an opinion as to which process option should be used.

What is more, from the selfish perspective of the work we do and the work we aspire to do, it is tempting to be directive. By providing a firm indication as to which process option we consider appropriate we are able to build the practice we want (and there are now many for whom court work is anathema and who will only undertake cases collaboratively). That decision making on the part of the lawyer is likely to be largely driven by self-interest, invariably from a commercial perspective of not wishing to lose the case to a mediator or if the collaborative process is chosen but fails.

As against that, ADR is about the client, not the lawyer. Lawyers should not be seeking to shape how they run their own practice to the detriment of clients. What is more, despite the emotional turmoil they may be going through, clients are truly best placed to make the right decision about process options. They know what makes their spouses tick, what are the issues which are central to resolution of the case and which option is most likely to work for the family. For many clients, it is empowering to have the autonomy of choosing a particular option. Ultimately, it is for clients to work through what are their own values and goals and to determine which option will likely work best in consequence.

3.6 CONCLUSION

As family lawyers, we recognise that there is not just one continuum. Most clients coming through our door for the first time will be divorcing for the first (and only) time; many will never have instructed a solicitor before. They will have a *War of the Roses* and *Kramer versus Kramer*-induced perception of divorce as being a very acrimonious process which will likely lead to courtroom drama. However, by educating clients in the whole range of process options available, we are showing that there does not inevitably have to be a painful journey leading to an externally imposed outcome in every case. Through this education, clients can move towards a continuum of other options, which is likely to have the benefits of preserving relations between the separating couple, maintaining confidentiality, reaching tailored solutions which are likely to be honoured by both parties, and containing costs. From the clients' perspective, they are likely to be grateful indeed for being shown that there is another way.

CHAPTER 4

Mediation

Emma Harte

4.1 WHAT IS MEDIATION?

Family mediation is a process in which a couple or family members, whether or not they are legally represented at any time, whether or not there are or have been any legal proceedings, agree to the appointment of a neutral third party (the mediator). The mediator is impartial and has no authority to make any decisions with regard to separation, divorce, children issues, property and finances, or any other issues that may be raised. A mediator should help the couple or family members reach their own informed decisions by negotiation and without adjudication.

4.1.1 Fundamental principles of mediation

There are a number of different models of mediation but there are some fundamental principles that can run through all models of mediation.

1. The use of a mediator

There cannot be mediation without a mediator. Mediation requires a third party to intervene impartially between the parties. It is this element of neutral third-party intervention that gives mediation its unique quality.

2. The mediator's impartiality

Impartiality or even-handedness is critical and implies being able to move one way or the other but always fairly and without overall favour.

3. The mediator's authority to determine the issues

A mediator cannot decide any issues for the parties. The mediator's job is to manage the process and help the parties reach their own decisions. The mediator's experience can of course benefit in this regard and help steer the parties to their decision.

4. Consensual resolution

The objective of mediation is that the parties themselves should agree on the outcome. The issues can only be said to be resolved when the parties have reached an agreement. If, at the end of a mediation, the parties cannot agree, the mediation will end any resolution (although often the issues will have been narrowed and the parties may be close to achieving an overall resolution) and the parties will be free to use another process.

5. Secure negotiation

All forms of mediation will normally provide a secure environment in which the mediation is conducted (i.e. secure in terms of the physical conditions and secure in terms of the mediation being confidential) with ground rules laid down to enable the parties to communicate freely to aid resolution.

4.1.2 The role of the mediator

The mediator has different roles within the process:

- **facilitator:** facilitating discussions;
- **manager:** managing the process;
- **information gatherer:** gathering all the financial disclosure where financial aspects need to be resolved;
- **information provider:** providing legal information and details, for instance about the Child Support Agency;
- **reality tester:** testing whether or not particular options are achievable in real life;
- **note taker:** making sure there is a note of the various options discussed and the issues raised and dealt with.

4.1.3 The basic stages of mediation

What does the mediator do when faced with an enquiry from a couple who potentially wish to take part in mediation?

There are essentially five stages involved in the mediation process.

Stage 1 – engaging the parties in the process

1. Have even-handed dealings on the telephone with both parties beforehand.
2. Inform both parties about the process, ground rules and that meetings normally take place with the mediator and the parties in the same room around the same table.
3. Discuss the process, procedure, costs and timing – not the merits.

4. Ensure there is no misunderstanding about the mediator's role.
5. Obtain names, addresses and contact numbers.
6. Check the urgency of the matter and the timetable involved.
7. Arrange a mediation appointment if required.
8. Send written information about the mediation process including the preliminary information form and the agreement to mediate. It is vital that the mediation agreement is signed before the mediation starts. It confirms the basis upon which the mediation will proceed and emphasises a number of the duties of the parties as well as confirming the confidential nature of the content of proposals made within mediation.

Stage 2 – obtaining commitment and agreeing rules (usually at first session)

1. Make sure the room and seating are appropriate (for example, check that the mediator is seated the same distance from each party).
2. Use the form of agreement to mediate.
3. Check all aspects of the agreement to mediate are understood and agreed, especially the confidentiality and privilege section. Note that it is clearly stated that all financial information is provided on an open basis which means that it can be used in court, but that discussions about possible terms of financial settlement are conducted on a *without prejudice* basis. Provisions about confidentiality and privilege will not apply, however, if any child or other person is suffering or likely to suffer significant harm.
4. Make sure the parties understand that substantive decisions are not binding until all parties have the opportunity to take advice from their solicitors.
5. Ask the parties to sign an agreement to mediate at the first session.
6. Consider the agenda, following receipt of the preliminary information form and further discussion.

Stage 3 – information gathering

Information is gathered by:

(a) use of initial information from discussion (use the preliminary information form);
(b) mediation financial statement (Form E) where financial issues are involved, together with supporting documents;
(c) probing; and
(d) appropriate use of a flip chart to ensure that the information is shared.

Stage 4 – facilitating discussions and negotiations

In order to facilitate discussions and negotiations between the parties, it is necessary for the mediator to:

- establish and develop a working agenda;
- help the couple to adopt a problem-solving approach;
- maintain future focus where possible;
- help the couple to consider the children and family;
- provide legal and other information but on an even-handed basis;
- identify, generate and list options, i.e. brainstorm with the couple;
- help the couple to explore, consider and prioritise options;
- assist the couple in testing the reality of different options and ideas;
- help the couple to communicate with each other;
- if necessary, help the parties to hear one another;
- allow ventilation of emotions to a degree but then bring the couple back to the issues;
- help the couple with their decision making, perhaps by suggesting short-term solutions where appropriate;
- assist sensible creativity and flexibility;
- maintain empathy and impartiality; and
- manage the process fairly and effectively but always be prepared to be firm where necessary.

Stage 5 – concluding the mediation

The mediation will come to an end when:

- issues are completely or partially resolved;
- either party wishes to terminate the mediation;
- both parties wish to terminate the mediation;
- the mediator wishes to terminate the process.

In most circumstances, thereafter, the mediator will usually prepare a summary (a memorandum of understanding), which the parties can then take to their respective solicitors for advice. The mediator's role may be built into a post-termination phase, however, so that the parties can revert as necessary on either the children or finance issues, depending on whether or not an agreement is reached.

4.2 MEDIATION SKILLS

There are a number of skills which the mediator must develop and use:

- effective listening;
- observing non-verbal communication, i.e. body language;
- helping the parties to hear one another;
- questioning (in order to obtain facts, find out about parties' concerns and see what needs to happen for those concerns to be addressed);

- summarising;
- acknowledging;
- neutralising (to maintain impartiality);
- normalising (if appropriate, explaining that it is common for the parties to feel or behave in this way in this situation);
- reframing (to make issues sound more palatable and not so personal to enable parties to move forward);
- managing conflict and venting of emotion;
- managing the process (the mediator must keep control of the mediation);
- lateral thinking (making alternative suggestions where appropriate); and
- encouraging a problem-solving mode – essential for making progress.

4.2.1 Dealing with emotions in mediation

It is very common for parties, both male and female, to show emotion, by way of tears, anger or otherwise and so the mediator should make this clear, i.e. normalise. The mediator should consider referring the couple to counselling if that is not already in place; while the mediator is to manage the process, he or she should be aware of his or her own limitations.

Ventilating of emotions is fine as long as it is controlled and is not abusive. The mediator should remind the parties of the ground rules agreed at the outset, and try to bring the parties back to focus on the central issues as soon as possible.

4.2.2 Power imbalances

Redress

Concern is sometimes expressed as to whether and how power imbalances between parties can effectively be redressed in mediation. These concerns are probably more prevalent in relation to family mediation, which may be perceived as benefiting the more powerful partner to the prejudice of the more vulnerable one. Although in fact either partner may be more powerful than the other, it is probably fair to say that a common stereotype in referring to these power imbalances is that of a powerful husband using mediation to dominate a weaker wife.

The nature and form of power

How does power arise in the relationship between a couple? An exhaustive list cannot be given but contributing factors may include the respective education and qualifications of each partner; the social standing of each partner; the financial standing of each of the partners and whether either is independent or dependent on the other, etc.; control or influence over financial affairs or children of the family; power exerted through threats; and the power of irrationality, i.e. the possibility that one will act unpredictably and irrationally with certain effects and consequences if a particular result is not achieved.

Dealing with power imbalances

It is not the mediator's function to try to change the power relationship between the parties for the future. However, an effective family mediation could have some impact on the power relationship between the parties.

It can be empowering for the less dominant party if the mediator helps the parties to communicate with one another more effectively so that they can address any issues which they may not have been able to express by themselves, and to deal in an orderly way with those issues. For example, it can be empowering for one person to be heard properly and have his or her views taken seriously, or for financial information to be shared in a way that may never have happened during the course of the relationship.

The mediator's responsibility is to ensure therefore that any power disparity that exists does not impact on the process in such a way as to make it unworkable and unfair. However, if an imbalance of power is impacting to the extent that it is making the process unfair, it will be necessary to terminate the mediation. Mediation is not appropriate for all couples by any means and the mediator needs to be constantly alert as to whether it would be fair to continue the process in each case on a session-by-session basis.

Potential violence or harm

Where power imbalance involves potential violence or harm, mediators must take particular care to establish whether mediation can take place at all, and if it can, under what circumstances and conditions. Cases of potential violence and harm should be identified as soon as possible – usually from the initial telephone calls to each party and from their completed preliminary information forms.

If mediation is to take place in a situation where one party is thought to be at any risk of harm by the other party, the mediator must take steps to try to ensure that both parties and the mediator are safe in the mediation. This should be addressed by, for example, appropriate arrangements for reception on arrival and for departure after the mediation, and by any other arrangements or conditions that the mediator may consider to be suitable.

Discussion of imbalances and establishing ground rules

By way of clarification, if a particular form of imbalance persists and it is impacting on the process, the mediator might decide to discuss this with the parties with a view to seeking some agreed formula for overcoming the problem, i.e. bring it into the open so that a way can be found to overcome it.

As a manager of the process, the mediator can stipulate ground rules to deal with any problems which may obstruct progress. It is a matter for the mediator whether this should be done by virtue of his or her authority or discussed and implemented by agreement with the parties.

If for example one party displays a tendency to interrupt and speak over the other, the mediator might make a specific rule to prevent this from happening. Alternatively, the mediator might discuss this with the parties, explaining that it is inhibiting progress and ask for authority from both of them to intervene should this occur again. Once both parties have given the mediator that specific authority, it becomes more difficult for an offending party to persist in the unhelpful conduct.

Other methods of reducing power imbalance

Power imbalances do not always have to be specifically discussed with the parties. For example, if one person has a greater control over the financial information than the other, this will be redressed by the procedures for providing and sharing relevant information.

It is generally accepted that having lawyers representing each party, as in the traditional process, helps to redress any power imbalances that exist between the parties. This is of course true in the main but many of the other power imbalances will remain.

4.2.3 Option development

The development of options is an essential element of mediation. It can be used in relation to all aspects, e.g. the future of the relationship, arrangements for the children and financial issues.

Options offer the couple ways of moving forward and may arise initially from the couple or the mediator. When exploring financial options it is often helpful to start with the issue of housing, as the remainder of the possible settlement terms will often flow from this.

4.2.4 Use of language

The choice of language is important in mediation. It is always necessary to think whether or not the language is:

- appropriate for the mediation;
- appropriate for the couple;
- too legalistic or formal;
- too colloquial or relaxed;
- too compassionate.

Questioning

A skilled mediator will be able to use questions quite cleverly. Questions are used:

- to gather information, get a better understanding of the issues and to probe aspects which are unclear;
- to get a party to test reality by confronting perceptions or positions with alternative ways of viewing the situation (this may be essential for understanding and movement);
- to promote reflection on any situation or proposal and to help a party to become more fully aware of the issues;
- to encourage a party to review a position or to focus on specific issues;
- to redirect the way in which discussions are moving;
- as a form of intervention in conflict management, to divert parties from a heated discussion into a more productive area.

A question may be strategic, where for instance the mediator knows the answer but wishes the party to arrive at the answer by himself or herself. Rather than expressing a personal view on a situation, the mediator can raise questions which allow parties to consider the issues needing to be examined without compromising the mediator's neutrality.

4.2.5 Impasse strategies

What does the mediator do when, as is often the case, both parties seem 'stuck' and neither can shift from their perspectives? There are various strategies which mediators use in such situations. For example, the mediator may:

- arrange for the parties to pause and consider;
- allow the couple time to absorb the progress;
- help underlying concerns or issues to surface;
- discuss unresolved emotional blocks;
- use caucusing – going between parties, perhaps with solicitors;
- address different perceptions of fairness;
- suggest short-term experiments to test different options;
- deal with conflicting advice from respective lawyers;
- consider obtaining counsel's advice on joint instructions
- prepare a summary of the position;
- examine the best and worst alternatives to an agreement;
- help the couple prepare for adjudication – including a discussion of what it will cost.

4.2.6 Summaries

It is often helpful to provide detailed summaries for the parties which they can each take back to their respective solicitors. Such summaries can then be used to help the solicitors to finalise the proposals and to draft the consent order. Summaries can:

- set out financial information with copies of supporting documentation;
- set out proposals made and the nature of without prejudice communications; and
- set out interim arrangements which are made without prejudice to further adjustment in the context of an overall resolution.

4.3 TERMINATING THE MEDIATION

The mediation can be terminated if:

- the couple reach consensus on all issues;
- the couple reach consensus on some issues and take the others to a different forum;
- the couple jointly decide to end the mediation without resolving the issues; or
- either party unilaterally decides to end the mediation.

Mediation can be suspended for a period of counselling, therapy or for solicitors to deal with certain interim issues.

Mediators can of course decide to end the mediation themselves where continuing the mediation is inappropriate, or where there is an abuse of process by either party, or where the conduct of either party is such that the mediation must be terminated.

4.4 SOLICITOR'S ROLE IN MEDIATION

In some models of family mediation, solicitors are not generally brought into the mediation process. In the Resolution model, mediation is conducted by and large without solicitors in attendance but there is a readiness to involve the parties' solicitors within the mediation process where this is appropriate and both the parties desire. The Resolution model encourages the parties to go back to their respective solicitors after each session so that they have suitable guidance the whole way through the process and, in particular, at the financial disclosure stage and at the stage where options are being discussed.

There are situations where the advice from a solicitor can make or break a mediation. Clients should be encouraged to take advice during a mediation and at the end of a mediation. On occasions this advice will be provided by the legal adviser being present within the mediation.

This can be a difficulty for solicitors who are being paid for through public funding because of the level of payment received. Where solicitors are to be involved in mediation, the mediator must consider whether this should be a 'same room' mediation, i.e. the clients, the solicitors and the mediator are all in the same room throughout or whether the mediation takes place using caucusing, i.e. an initial session with all parties and their solicitors and then each client occupies a separate room with their solicitor and the mediator shuttles between the solicitors and their clients. If the latter, the mediator must be clear with their clients what information is to be conveyed to the other side, i.e. should it be all information including all proposals, or only some information and some proposals. If the solicitors are present and an outcome is achieved the solicitors will generally draft the outcome (consent order or separation agreement).

The solicitors can also have a role in mediation by providing advice to their clients. This is commonly given in a letter to the client; sometimes this is produced during the course of the mediation and offered to the mediator. The mediator must be careful not to read the correspondence since anything which the mediator receives should be conveyed to the other party and there may be confidential or privileged content in the letter. On occasions the client is given advice verbally by the solicitor and the advice as conveyed within the mediation seems to have been misunderstood or unlikely. In such situations the mediator may wish to clarify the advice with the solicitor either verbally or in writing.

There is also scope for flexibility and the ability to deal with matters in the way in which civil or commercial mediations proceed. These (and other) options are discussed by Neil Robinson in **Chapter 6**.

CHAPTER 5

The collaborative process

Emma Harte and James Pirrie

5.1 INTRODUCTION

Collaborative practice is a relatively new model of resolving family disputes outside litigation. In short, each client is represented by a separate, independent solicitor and both clients and solicitors attend meetings together (*four-way meetings*) to try to resolve matters. The fundamental principle is that no court proceedings are permitted while the collaborative process is ongoing.

Both clients sign a binding participation agreement which precludes the solicitors from participating in litigation between the parties. There is a commitment to:

- early and full disclosure;
- good faith bargaining rather than positional bargaining;
- respect for the other party.

Both solicitors agree to withdraw if either party issues an application with the court and thereafter new solicitors have to be instructed by both parties. This is to keep everyone at the negotiating table in the face of an apparent impasse.

The collaborative process is family centred and about what is best for that particular family rather than trying to achieve the best financial outcome for a client.

All successful collaborative lawyers have recognised the need in many cases for a second professional – the family consultant – to provide a support service that will help the clients to address the non-legal agenda (i.e. all the practical issues regarding the children and any emotional or relationship issues) and help the clients deal with the four-way negotiations.

5.2 THE COLLABORATIVE LAWYER

Collaborative lawyers (when acting in a collaborative capacity) can do everything that a conventional and traditional family lawyer does except initiate and pursue contested court proceedings. The collaborative model is also now being used in civil and commercial disputes.

The difference between mediation and the collaborative process is that in the collaborative model, each party has legal advice at all times during the process. Even if, for instance, one client lacks financial understanding, this power imbalance is rectified by the direct participation of the lawyers. If the clients are being unreasonable, it is the job of the lawyers to work with their own clients in order to ensure that the process remains productive. The participation or collaborative agreement also requires a lawyer to withdraw from the process on becoming aware that his or her client is not being frank or open or is participating in the process in bad faith. The same is true if the client fails to honour agreements made during the course of the negotiations.

Collaborative lawyers are specifically trained to help their clients achieve the best possible outcome for their families as opposed to achieving the largest possible financial award for a particular client. Collaborative lawyers encourage the highest good faith problem-solving behaviour from their own clients and from themselves. Collaborative lawyers are skilled in finding solutions that can be accepted by both clients.

Trust between the lawyers is essential for the collaborative process to work. In addition, collaborative practice demands specialist skills from the lawyers in guiding negotiations and managing conflict. It is critical therefore that both lawyers participating in the process are properly trained in collaborative law. It is not possible, for example, to work collaboratively with the other lawyer but still go to court if the process is not successful. It is felt that if the lawyers can still consider unilateral resort to the court as a fall back position, their thought processes are hampered. Only when everyone involved knows that it is down to the four of them to think of a solution (otherwise the process will fail and the lawyers will be disqualified from continuing to act), does the collaborative model actually work. All four need to take responsibility for finding an acceptable solution.

5.3 OTHER MEMBERS OF THE COLLABORATIVE TEAM

The role, qualifications and responsibilities of others in the collaborative process are covered in detail in **Chapter 7**, so these are only summarised here. Most family law practitioners, in their traditional work, will refer clients to counselling and mediation services wherever appropriate. The collaborative process recognises that other support (aside from the guidance from the lawyers) is often very helpful, if not crucial, if clients are to be able to deal with all the emotional and relationship issues involved in the breakdown of a relationship as well as children issues. As noted above, such support may be needed to help clients cope with the four-way negotiations. This support can often be provided at a lower cost, notwithstanding the perceived extra cost of involving additional professionals such as the family consultant.

The family consultant is known as a 'coach' in the United States. Typically, the family consultant will be a counsellor or therapist and often also a mediator and will be involved by a referral from one or both of the lawyers involved in the collaborative process.

The family consultant might be involved in supporting one party only (i.e. each party might have his or her own family consultant) or, alternatively, just one family consultant may be used to help both clients to deal with children arrangements and to facilitate better communication between them.

Family consultants are the professionals most commonly brought into the process but others may be involved including:

- accountants to assist with tax implications or with valuations of businesses and shares;
- independent financial advisers to provide information about mortgages and insurance policies, etc.;
- financial assistants to help with tasks such as preparing budgets, but at a lower cost to the clients than a lawyer;
- actuaries to deal with pension issues.

5.4 STAGES OF THE COLLABORATIVE PROCESS

5.4.1 The initial stage – first meeting with the client

It is essential for all the options to be explained to the client, i.e. whether to mediate, negotiate in the traditional process or to deal with matters in the collaborative process. It is important to bear in mind that mediation and the collaborative process are not suitable for everyone and it is only right therefore that the clients know what to expect from each process so that they can gauge whether they can cope with it and make informed choices. Information on the various processes should be given to the client so that they can take it away to read at home, and Resolution publishes a number of useful pamphlets in this regard (see also **Chapter 3**). Very often this leads to clients discussing the collaborative option with their spouse or partner and if both parties are interested, a second collaborative lawyer can be found through the Resolution website (**www.resolution.org.uk**). Alternatively, the client could ask the lawyer to provide the POD's brochure (see p. 61), or a list of names of suitable collaborative lawyers from whom the spouse can choose.

The collaborative lawyers then make contact and preparations to proceed are put in place.

It is at this point that anchor or aspiration statements will be drafted. As Gillian Bishop described in *A Client's Guide to Collaborative Divorce* (FLiP, 2010), the anchor statement sets out why the client wants to resolve the issues collaboratively; how the process will work for them and their family; what solutions the financial outcome will offer them and their family; and, where applicable, how the co-parenting relationship will work post-divorce or separation. These statements help break an impasse by the parties reverting to them at times of difficulty and also help set the scene in creating a proper and true collaborative atmosphere in the room. The statements are best put forward in an optimistic tone, expressing commitment to the process.

5.4.2 The first two-way discussion between lawyers

It is the lawyer's job to manage the process and this will include sharing information such as potential issues or stumbling blocks that are likely to be faced and whether or not the clients will benefit from family consultancy, the assistance of accountants, advice from independent financial advisers, etc. Usually this two-way discussion will take place over the telephone and practical arrangements for the forthcoming four-way meeting with clients will be made.

5.4.3 The client and lawyer two-way meeting

The lawyer will want the client to go into the four-way meeting well prepared. There should be no real surprises for anyone at the first four-way meeting, and family consultancy and the introduction of any financial experts will often be discussed with clients at this stage.

5.4.4 The first four-way meeting

The aim of this first meeting is to ensure that the clients understand the process and appreciate their responsibilities within it. The participation agreement will be the main focus and this will be signed by the lawyers and the clients if everyone is satisfied that it is the best way forward for the clients given the issues involved.

As stated earlier, the participation agreement binds the clients to behave courteously and prevents them from beginning any contested proceedings during the course of the collaborative process. It also prevents the lawyers from ever acting on behalf of the clients in any contested proceedings. This typically makes everyone work harder to ensure that the negotiations work. Very few clients will want to start again on another process with fresh lawyers and all the costs that would be entailed.

5.4.5 The continuation of the process

Commonly, the collaborative lawyers are engaged primarily in trying to resolve the financial issues (whilst perhaps the children issues are dealt with through mediation) and so there may be a slight gap before the second meeting while each client prepares and collates their financial disclosure using Form E, although this is not always the case. By the time the second four-way meeting begins, there will have been an exchange of financial information and the lawyers can then begin to explore and discuss various options with the clients within the four-way meeting. The four-way meetings will continue with the lawyers and clients preparing for each four-way in advance. The two lawyers will also often have discussions in between four-way meetings to consider how best to manage the process so as to achieve an early resolution. When an agreement is reached, in due course, the lawyers can then turn it into a consent order in the usual way to be submitted to the court for approval and sealing.

5.4.6 Dealing with an impasse

It is inevitable that from time to time the collaborative lawyers and their respective clients will become 'stuck'. There are a number of ways to deal with these *stuck* positions.

1. It can be helpful for the lawyers to be open as to their views on how a court might deal with the situation. If their views differ, this can only highlight the risk that the clients will take if they decide to litigate as different judges will probably also have differing views and in the light of this, compromises may be made.
2. The costs of litigation (financial and personal) can be estimated and very often this will help to promote a settlement.
3. The collaborative lawyers could bring in a mediator on a civil and commercial model basis, i.e. with the mediator caucusing between each collaborative lawyer and their respective client. Sometimes a fresh approach is needed and an impartial mediator could be exactly the external influence needed to assist.
4. A further option is for the collaborative lawyers to consider obtaining counsel's opinion on joint instructions. This is often a good way of promoting a settlement particularly when counsel is very experienced, and commands respect.

5.4.7 Concluding the process

This is dealt with more fully in **Chapter 11** but, essentially, the process will conclude when an agreement is reached which is then turned into a consent order to be submitted to the court for approval and sealing, or when the process is terminated by one or both clients, or one or both lawyers, before an agreement is reached.

5.5 THE GIVING OF ADVICE IN THE COLLABORATIVE PROCESS

No restriction on giving advice applies to the collaborative lawyer such as that which exists for mediators. After all, the collaborative lawyer engages in the collaborative process as a representative for his or her client and with that partisan responsibility intact – if modified by the instructions the clients each give the lawyers in the participation agreement.

Collaborative lawyers are encouraged to think beyond the traditional professional approach to giving advice, which might be caricatured as:

- obtain the relevant facts;
- inform the client about the relevant legal principles;
- advise the client as to the likely application of principles to facts;
- help them to gain an understanding as to the costs and uncertainties; and
- take the negotiations forward . . .

. . . *anything better than this is a win.*

The collaborative process endeavours to give voice to the client's aspirations and values (rather than values of the courts), so it is hardly surprising that it encourages us to downplay the legal prognosis. However, some have interpreted that as suggesting that advice should never be given, on the basis that once given, advice would provide a dangerous and beguiling 'slit trench' into which the individual would slip, leading to the adoption of positional bargaining, so toxic to the ethic of interest-based negotiation that collaborative practice aims to promote.

But that is inconsistent with our duties as family lawyers (if we are free of family law, we are really failing to do what is written on our tin). If the collaborative process really is about informed self-determination then it cannot be without appropriate and timely advice. Our clients cannot be informed if we are denying them an understanding of the alternative, so we have a fundamental duty to advise them – and, indeed, we are probably negligent if we allow them to go forward without it. The key then becomes the timing of when the advice is given – and the differentiation between advising on legal principles and applying those principles once articulated.

A potential danger here is the client who thinks we have *the answer*, which will unlock the outcome to the case, and all they have to do is work out which buttons to press to get us to produce the goods.

The process in these circumstances is likely to be characterised by client frustration as they peck for the answer, diverting everyone's attention from the task at hand: the clients finding their own solutions with the lawyers' assistance.

There is a great difference between telling a client, 'you are entitled to x and I will get it for you', and discussing the legal principles that seem to be engaged in their situation. There is value in explaining principles at an early stage, and some that exist within the law (e.g. best interests of children, acquest and needs-based resolution of financial questions) contain a great deal of common sense, so clients may want to adopt them within their mix of values.

We do not, however, dive straight into our views of outcome the minute we sit down in our first collaborative meeting. If we did so, most clients would also dive straight to claim the grounds of their rights and we could not move forward. If the best way of helping clients move forward is to focus on their positive aspirations then it is hardly going to be helpful to tell them that, whatever their aspirations, they ought to be fitting in within a framework.

It is also unlikely to work so far as the professionals are concerned. We are likely to go back to the day job and harden in our views about what the right sort of outcome ought to look like. It is then bound to stop being the client's process (which is after all what we have promoted) and become a legal scrap, with the clients spectating from the sidelines.

However, clear legal information may be needed at the point where the clients have started to run out of ideas and are drifting towards, 'if you can't see it my way there's a chance that we may have to sort it out with *proper* lawyers'. This is where the clients need to get the idea that there may well be no better court solution; that they are already each better off than they would be if they went down that route; that progress is being made; and that 'it's difficult because it is' – it will not be any easier when this difficulty is articulated (in about 18 months' time) in a court.

The lawyers at that point can reignite the process, reflecting on the bracket of outcome. If the lawyers agree then that is interesting and may be helpful (it may even provide the bridge to fill the gap), but they tend not to. They tend to be some distance apart from each other and what the clients start to see (and it is a wonderful moment to watch) is that despite their experience, even they don't know the answer and the outcome is unpredictable.

Often the law has no answers for the clients to bridge the final gap – they have already taken the solution a distance away from legal norms, and the language of court-style solutions is likely to be foreign to the discussions advancing at the collaborative table.

Factoring in likely costs, clients pretty quickly realise that there is no externally imposed option that is viable for them to pursue and they both need to get back to the job of sorting out a deal.

This is what we mean by 'legal advice within the collaborative process'. It is not prescriptive, but provides the background to the conversation. It articulates the principles, and possibly the parameters of the conversation, and can be effective at illustrating why a block has been reached, highlighting the obstacles to overcoming it through the traditional route. After all, as Ian Hislop delights in saying, 'in any court case, at least 50% of the lawyers are always wrong!'

5.6 COLLABORATIVE 'LITE'

Collab-lite starts out by sounding like a winner for all. An agreement may be written to commit all in the room to being constructive. Clients seem to have purchased a process that will rescue them from the toxicity and expense of the court process. There is no exclusion clause – in the event of breakdown of the collaborative process, the lawyers would be free to carry on with the case and the parties would be free to continue to use them. Lawyers win – clients win . . . where is the harm? Supporters of collab-lite argue that it is in the client's interests to retain the lawyer of their choice and to avoid the additional costs of a new lawyer starting afresh.

5.6.1 What are the rules of engagement?

In any quasi-collaborative process where the lawyer can continue to act for the client in court proceedings, the golden rule of the true collaborative process is breached. A lawyer can hear the other client's innermost thoughts, wishes, values, hopes and fears. The lawyer will have gained an advantage in knowing how to cross-examine that client later purely as a result of the client being honest on the understanding that the meetings are confidential and without prejudice. That client will feel betrayed by the process and those involved in it if the other lawyer can threaten and then issue court proceedings. This is compounded by the lawyer cross-examining them in those proceedings.

Are the supporters of collab-lite prepared to frontload their process by correctly informing the clients that the other lawyer can cross-examine them later? If not, then a client will feel they were not informed by their own lawyer about the full implications of being able to retain their lawyers. If the clients are properly informed then the natural result will be that clients will not be open and forthcoming in the four-way process.

Accordingly, we see the harm as lying in the fact that clients are much *less* likely to win. If they do skate across the pond to a set of solutions on the far bank, they are likely to have got there on ice that was pretty thin at certain points and certainly, if they fall through, there will be far fewer resources to help them manage the accident well.

Presumably in collab-lite lawyers can twin-track with the court process. Whether or not they do, the commitment to the work at the table risks being half-hearted. If things get tough, there will be pull out, into the *certainty* of the court. That option undermines the chance of the client getting to the better solutions at the collaborative table.

It is very hard (given that the hard edges of the court process are just over the hedge) in the collab-lite process to avoid using the threat of court – but such threats will undermine progress in the collaborative process. Where that threat exists, then increasingly court principles and outcomes are going to seep into the discussions.

The clients are going to edge away from doing the work that they could do in finding their own solutions and will rely more upon the lawyer and the 'magic' of law-based solutions. (We know of course that such law-based solutions usually have at least two answers and the gap in between is often a large one to bridge whilst maintaining goodwill.)

We believe too that there is a profound risk to the professional. With the close presence of legal process, that is the prevailing ethic. We know many behaviours that are not acceptable in the collaborative process would be treated as normal in a court-based process. In the cordial atmosphere of the four-way meeting, we are likely to let our guard slip, exposing our client to disadvantage if our collab-lite colleague decides that their client's interests dictate that they exploit the vulnerability. We are likely to be left exposed, with the professional relationship in tatters and with a disappointed client or worse on our hands.

For all these reasons, we feel that collab-lite does not give clients the best chance of reaching a good agreement.

However, there are times when we cannot avoid what is, in effect, collab-lite. For example, currently those with less than three years' family law experience cannot train and not all solicitors of over three years' experience are trained. Here we cannot collaborate. There are also the cases where one or other (or both) teams are uncertain whether the collaborative process is suitable. They want to explore the dynamics of meeting together, and to see whether the doubts that may exist materialise. An agreement may be reached not to sign the participation agreement at the first meeting. What are, therefore, the rules of that game? The clients may well see this as part of the collaborative process, without stepping through the wardrobe into collaborative Narnia, but at least having a peep through the door. The temptation thereafter may be never to sign up ('we are doing ok without it so why bother?'), but with the participants nevertheless believing that they are collaborating. If the sequence of meetings fails, it will be broadcast to family, friends and new non-collaborative lawyers as a collaborative failure, when it never was.

Collaborative practitioners should be protectors of the brand. They and their clients must be clear as to what process they are using. Unless or until a participation agreement has been signed by everyone, the '*c* word' should not be used. In our view, that is where the term *collab-lite* falls down. If the lawyers can be retained in contested proceedings then it is not a collaborative case – it is a round-table negotiation.

CHAPTER 6

Developing the mediation model

Neil Robinson

Rules and models destroy genius and art. (William Hazlitt, 18th-century essayist)

6.1 INTRODUCTION

Whilst the fundamental principles and process of mediation were explored in **Chapter 4**, its essential qualities also include flexibility and variety, genius and art. There is now a greater readiness among alternative (or appropriate) dispute resolution (ADR) professionals to explore different ways of working, to adapt accepted processes and models, and to work with other professionals. This chapter explores:

- working with civil or hybrid models;
- models of partnership of mediators and lawyers; and
- the implications of integration into Children Act proceedings.

It provides questions and challenges, rather than formulaic answers, in keeping with the dynamic nature of ADR (as opposed to litigation). Although the focus here is on how mediation might be developed, much of what is said about the need to develop and be more flexible is as valid for collaborative law and other models.

6.2 SOME BASIC PRINCIPLES

6.2.1 Why should mediation develop?

There are a number of advantages to developing mediation models in family matters:

1. A core belief of mediators is that people in conflict can, and should, be given every opportunity to work together to resolve their disputes cooperatively, for their own sakes and for the good of their children and society. A core expectation of courts should be that the potential for cooperative resolution has been definitively assessed.

2. The greater the level of conflict, the greater the imperative to find a mediated solution, the greater the rewards of doing so, and the greater differential in outcome.
3. In principle, any dispute, at any stage of litigation, is potentially suitable for mediation, with appropriate judicial oversight (see Thorpe LJ in *Al-Khatib* v. *Masry* [2004] EWCA Civ 1353, [2005] 1 FLR 381).
4. Effective ADR in complex and entrenched cases is likely to involve working in partnership with other professional colleagues and the court process – a far more evolved multidisciplinary approach than we have previously embraced.
5. If the parties want to attempt to work cooperatively, if there is a public interest in them doing so, but the traditional models will not fit, we have an obligation to examine whether an alternative, bespoke model can be created.
6. Therefore, the job of the family mediator is to expand, not limit, those areas where mediation might effectively be used to resolve disputes. The question must be, not 'Does this problem fit my model of ADR?' but, instead, 'Is it in the interests of this family to resolve their conflicts cooperatively? If so, can I provide a cost-effective process that will give the parties the opportunity to achieve this?' That is, the mediator must develop the process to meet the needs of the clients, rather than expect them to conform to a rigid model.
7. The effectiveness of the mediation will depend upon the commitment of the parties, the creativity and experience of the mediators, their understanding and knowledge of the context, and the establishment of agreed boundaries, ground rules and processes through the negotiation of an agreement between the mediators and the participants.
8. The most effective mediation services in the future will be those that can offer a wide range of flexible models, perhaps in addition to other ADR services ranging from collaborative law to parenting classes.

6.2.2 Mediation as jazz

Both mathematics and jazz have been described as spontaneous invention within a theoretical framework, a description that might equally apply to mediation. That spontaneous invention is probably what draws us to be ADR professionals and which gives the clients the opportunity to create cooperative solutions. But what is the fundamental theoretical framework within which we might spontaneously invent, and outside which it would not be mediation?

The four principles of mediation remain impartiality, voluntariness, confidentiality and clients' decision making. If these are compromised, what remains may not be mediation but may be a new form of ADR. So, for example, hybrid models of mediation can still be described as mediation, but will probably require a modification of the agreement to mediate or mediation terms and ground rules. Court-directed ADR (see **6.5** below), and In-court Conciliation delivered by the Child and Family Court Advisory and Support Service (CAFCASS) could not be 'family mediation' as defined in the UK by lead body codes of practice such as that of Resolution.

It is therefore important to distinguish variations which:

- fall inside a standard agreement to mediate;
- may require modification of an agreement to mediate;
- are no longer recognisably or fundamentally mediation.

These four principles provide the key to successful mediation. Those cases where the principles have to be compromised provide an additional challenge to the ADR specialist – how to re-incorporate the essence of those principles wherever possible. An example might be the active participation of lawyers in a mediator-led settlement meeting or quasi-financial dispute resolution. One of the dangers here is that the clients start to lose control over the decision making, so the mediator will have to be vigilant in maintaining a process that allows the ownership of negotiation and decision making to remain with the clients.

6.2.3 Preparation

An assessment as to suitability therefore needs to include an assessment as to the most appropriate model of ADR. One might create a pro forma as an assessment tool, e.g. to:

1. Identify the expectations and commitment of the parties.
2. Identify the subject matter of the dispute.
3. Consider the level of entrenchment and/or complexity.
4. Assess possible risks, abuse and power.
5. Identify the aims and objectives of the process.
6. Identify the position reached within the court process, and how information is to be exchanged or others actively involved.
7. Design and define the tailor-made model.
8. Discuss and agree with parties and any representatives transparently.
9. Modify any agreement to mediate to take account of this, and agree any additional ground rules.
10. Discuss with a professional practice consultant (PPC).

6.2.4 Some variations on the mediation model

When selecting the most appropriate model, one needs to take into account variations of subject matter, format and participants:

- How therapeutic is the model? – Mediation models can be called problem-solving, bargaining, narrative or transformative – that is, is the process focused solely on reaching agreement or on digging deeper, sharing the stories, and transforming the relationships?

- How far should the mediator intervene? – Level of evaluation, direction, or shift to arbitration.
- How many mediators? – Co-mediation, sole mediation, anchor.
- Does the mediator hold secrets? – Joint and/or private meetings, shuttle, caucus (see **6.3.6**).
- How does the subject matter determine the model used? – Hybrid, civil models (e.g. Trusts of Land and Appointment of Trustees Act (TOLATA) 1996 cases) (see **6.3.4**).
- Frequency and length of meetings.
- Active participation of lawyers or other professionals in the mediation process.
- Direct or indirect involvement of children and/or others.
- Court-directed ADR: the mediation service is the jointly instructed expert.
- Agreement concluded in mediation or deferred.
- Limited objectives – shared history, full disclosure.
- Tele-mediation – video, telephone and online dispute resolution.
- Cross-border/international/cross-cultural ADR processes.

An open-minded consideration of these variations in the context of the checklist at **6.2.3** should assist the mediator to find the best model to serve the parties' needs.

A note about evaluation and direction

Evaluation by both clients and mediators is a necessary part of mediation, if only in the form of reality-testing options. Lawyer mediators may extend this to a consideration of whether certain proposals would fall within reasonable parameters. An element of direction is often necessary in children cases, for example with young, inexperienced parents. If this were to extend to a more formal evaluation or arbitration, it would not meet the accepted definition of family mediation. There has however been limited development of models of 'med-arb', where the mediator adopts a semi-adjudicative role. There is clearly potential for the further development of such a model, although detailed consideration falls outside the scope of this chapter.

6.2.5 Warning – modifying the model, not breaking the mould

To be unclear about the purpose of the creative intervention is to risk chaos. The more the process is developed in an individual case, the more critical it becomes for it to be transparently specified, for those boundaries and ground rules to be agreed and for the basic mediation principles to be upheld.

Balance and proportion are essential; it is important not go beyond experience and expertise or too far outside the comfort zone. Support by way of a co-mediator and open-minded professional practice consultant will also be required.

6.3 COMBINING THE CIVIL AND FAMILY MEDIATION MODELS

6.3.1 Development of civil and family models

Civil and family mediation models have developed in very different ways over the last 20 years. There are good reasons for this divergence, but much would be gained now by revisiting many of the differences. The challenge arises from:

(a) those mediations where the subject matter straddles the jurisdictions;
(b) high conflict cases, where existing models drawn solely from one profession are inadequate;
(c) the increasing volume and maturity of mediation, and the scope for real learning, understanding and evolution.

6.3.2 Is the ethical base of civil mediation essentially different from that of family mediation?

Family mediation, especially where there are children, is in essence about transformation of relationships from antagonism to cooperation. Civil mediation is more often an alternative, more cost-effective, pragmatic, form of adversarial litigation.

In the civil model lawyers play a central part, and they may adopt as adversarial a stance as in litigation. In family mediations, there is seen to be added value in the parties preserving a relationship (particularly where there are children or some other continuing common interest such as a shared business, or a historical or family context to preserve), and in working together at a common problem.

At its simplest, civil mediation may be a continuation of the contest, albeit on different rules and territory, whereas family mediation is about seeking effective rearrangement of family systems and resources.

6.3.3 The essential differences between family and civil mediation models

This may explain how civil and family models have developed so differently. Any of these differences is open to detailed discussion as to whether the distinctive elements remain justifiable. For example, what about the different approach to provision of documents? Or the (non-)binding nature of settlement proposals? To the open-minded, creative mediator seeking to find common ground between these approaches, these issues are brought into stark

Table 6.1 Civil, family and hybrid models of mediation

	Typical civil	Typical family	Typical hybrid
1.	Takes place over the course of a day or longer, or part of a day	Takes place over a series of meetings, a few weeks apart	Either/both
2.	Caucused in separate rooms, starting and interspersed with joint meetings	Usually in the same room; increasing minority shuttled	Either/both
3.	Mediators hold separate confidences	Mediators and parties share everything, even if shuttled	Either/both
4.	Mediators have pleadings or case statements	Mediators may not have access to court or legal documents	Either/both
5.	No pre-mediation assessment and screening	Follows assessment process and screening	Unclear – either?
6.	Solicitors present except in low value cases	Solicitors not present	Either/both
7.	Results in binding agreement and Tomlin order	Results in confidential summary given effect by lawyers or court	Unclear – either?
8.	Mediator impartial, but may suggest proposals or privately indicate their views	Mediator impartial, and will not usually evaluate or be directive	Either/both
9.	Typically undertaken by individual mediators, who may be lawyers or from other commercial professions	Typically undertaken by members of mediation services in the professional or charitable sectors	May depend on whether pre-/ post-proceedings
10.	Typically referred by court or solicitors to one of a panel of mediators taken from national or regional organisations	Typically referred by solicitor or self-referred by parties to named mediation service	Mediators can come from both sides of profession
11.	Unregulated so far, but mediators generally members of either CEDR or ADR Group; currently various initiatives for registration or regulation underway	Regulated, in that all mediators practising publicly funded work are accredited and supervised at least as rigorously as family lawyers	Depends on 9. above
12.	Voluntary, but increasingly under pressure of costs sanctions	Voluntary, but triggered by Funding Code referral in publicly funded cases or 'contact activity direction'	As above
13.	May take place before, or following stay of litigation	Generally takes place before, but increasingly, alongside, litigation	Either/both
14.	Privately funded, but increasingly may be under terms of insurance	Privately or publicly funded	Opportunities for both private and public funding

relief when a case is referred that appears to straddle the jurisdictions. **Table 6.1** sets out the defining features of the typical family and civil models, and adds a third column for devising a hybrid.

Notes to Table 6.1

- Virtually all civil cases start with a joint meeting, to which they return from time to time. However, negotiation typically takes place between separate camps, unlike the family model.
- Typically the family process is one stretching over weeks, whereas civil cases are usually resolved over one continuous session.
- Civil mediations use the mediator's ability to hold confidences about parties' positions (caucusing) whereas family mediators generally consider it inappropriate to hold secrets even when shuttling.
- Policy about provision of documents varies widely in family mediation, and increasingly documents are provided in cases of complexity. Civil mediations will almost invariably be assisted by the provision of mediation case statements, and often pleadings and bundles.
- Whilst no formal screening or assessment (such as in family cases) takes place in civil mediation, there is substantial pre-mediation process activity.
- The area of suggesting proposals, evaluation or direction in mediation is controversial but it is probably more common for civil mediators to express private views on the merits.
- The choice of mediator in the commercial field is much more complex; court schemes vary, some use judges themselves (the Technical and Construction Court scheme) and others use provider organisations.
- There is currently much change and debate about regulation and registration in the civil arena.
- There is research in both civil and family jurisdictions suggesting that pressure to mediate may be counterproductive – see, e.g. *Twisting arms: court referred and court linked mediation under judicial pressure* (Dame Hazel Genn, 21 May 2007, **www.justice.gov.uk/publications/research210507.htm**).

6.3.4 A hybrid mediation model

A model could be created for a specific case that uses elements from both accepted models. Whatever we devise for our third column will be transparently constructed and specified, adopting those aspects of each model that are most likely to assist.

Just as all cases lie somewhere on a spectrum of levels of conflict, so it can be argued that all (family) conflicts lie at a unique point on a spectrum from commercial bargain to ongoing relationship or communication. So a model of mediation that draws on the best of both pure family and civil models is likely to be suitable for any of the following where:

(a) the subject matter straddles jurisdictions – TOLATA 1996, inheritance, etc.;
(b) the subject matter is complex, such as where there are substantial shared or overlapping business interests and shareholdings, multiple properties, or complex pension arrangements;
(c) the conflict requires something more robust than the standard family approach, but the level of ongoing relationship requires more than an arm's length civil model;
(d) there are many parties to the dispute.

A starting place for constructing that model might be an analysis of where our case lies on each of these spectra (see **Figure 6.1** below).

EXAMPLE 1: Intergenerational farming litigation

The final hearing in Chancery proceedings over respective interests in a family farm was stayed pending mediation between the four parties, two of whom were divorcing spouses in ancillary relief proceedings, themselves adjourned generally pending the outcome of the Chancery proceedings. Total costs to date in the four-year-long proceedings were over £30,000. Following separate assessment meetings, a hybrid family/civil mediation took place lasting one day, attended by the four parties and their solicitors and counsel. A Tomlin order was concluded in the Chancery proceedings, and a publicly funded privileged family mediation also produced a memorandum of understanding in respect of the ancillary relief proceedings. The total cost to the four parties and the public purse was just over £2,000.

EXAMPLE 2: Inheritance claim in civil proceedings

Mediation took place over a day between the claimant widowed mother claiming a share in the estate left by her estranged deceased husband to three

Subject matter

Civil claim<--->family dispute

Desired outcome

Commercial bargain<---------------------------------->ongoing relationship

Complexity/conflict

High conflict<--->financial complexity

Figure 6.1 Spectrum of conflict

children, who were themselves at different stages of estrangement from the mother. Although the basic model used to reach settlement was solicitor-supported civil mediation, a flexible approach was used to allow joint meetings (sometimes between family members with the support of the mediator but not the lawyers) to deal with the sensitivities of the issues, the interplay of family and civil law and practice and the prospect of ongoing relationships following the resolution, resulting in a Tomlin order.

6.3.5 A specific area – mediating cohabitants

Typically, separating cohabitants seeking mediation pre-proceedings find themselves referred by family lawyers to family mediators (especially if they are publicly funded). Yet once proceedings have started, the referral to mediation, if any, is from civil proceedings to civil mediators. This distinction seems arbitrary and hard to justify. The existence of a hybrid model to deal with both economic and relationship issues would benefit all.

Where do cohabitation disputes lie on the spectra above? It may be that the end of the cohabitation is like the end of a business relationship, but, more likely, especially if there are children, there will be issues over emotions, continuing relationship and communications to be untangled, for which the skills of the family mediator would be as essential as in divorce. So a model is needed that is flexible enough to accommodate this.

Why mediate?

Many of the arguments for mediating divorce disputes surely apply with greater force in cohabitation cases, where there is huge uncertainty about the state of the law and the costs of litigation are significantly higher. This is supported by Thorpe LJ in *W* v. *W (Joinder of Trusts of Land Act and Children Act Applications)* [2003] EWCA Civ 924, [2004] 2 FLR 321, a TOLATA 1996 case which encourages the consideration of all issues together, the predominance of children issues, and the use of mediation.

For the reasons set out above about the ethical base of each pure model, there would seem to be strong reason for family mediators to take such cases on.

Possible models

Depending on the level of conflict, and the balance between need for simple commercial bargain or ongoing relationship, decisions could be made about one-day or multi-session process, lawyers in or out, same room or caucus, and so on.

As to documentation, the sharing of information or open financial summary would need explicit modification to allow for relevant and proportionate, not comprehensive, disclosure about issues such as a shared history of contributions and intentions.

Similarly, the structure of a memorandum of understanding is likely to be significantly different. What is the legal status of such a document? And, if a mediated agreement leading to a Tomlin order is negotiated by civil mediators, how adequate will this be if there are children or relationship issues?

6.3.6 Shuttling family mediation

Another fundamental difference in models is whether mediation takes place in the same room or not. For some family mediators, working in separate rooms is anathema; it is *simply not mediation*.

Dangers

There are plenty of reasons to be cautious and sceptical:

1. If the factors militating against face-to-face meeting are so great, why mediate at all?
2. If the ills are absence of trust, abuse or power imbalance, how are they to be cured without face-to-face communication?
3. If mediation is about accentuating the positive, does shuttling not preserve the negative?
4. Is this anything more than arm's length negotiation, but quicker?

There are dangers for mediators themselves here, including:

- a shooting the messenger scenario;
- setting up unrealistic expectations;
- an onus on the mediator to report accurately;
- the process may take longer and be more costly;
- it can encourage entrenchment;
- it can be stressful;
- the possibility of letting the ground rules slide;
- keeping the unengaged party interested;
- balancing the time.

Benefits

However, if the parties wish to work towards a cooperative conclusion, but are unable to meet together, the mediator should not refuse the parties the opportunity. At the very least shuttling might be an appropriate model to support a commercial bargaining process along civil lines, or to model communication where a face-to-face meeting is impossible.

This is a difficult balance. For example, if mutual distrust underlies a contact dispute, it is difficult to see how shuttled mediation might assist; but where communication is essential, it may provide a bridge to something better, as an attempt to model better communication.

Other benefits might be:

- it could lead to work in the same room;
- it may be the only way to keep the process going;
- it avoids imbalances and may be less stressful;
- there is the opportunity for individual empathy;
- it provides the opportunity to explore options with the mediator without commitment or raising expectations;
- it gives the parties the space to breathe and think privately.

Safeguards

Safeguards can be put in place including:

- keeping track of time, keeping participants informed, transparency about the process both in the sessions and in the outcome summary;
- the use of co-mediating;
- revising the agreement to mediate;
- establishing realistic expectations;
- establishing ground rules through the involvement of lawyers;
- effective planning, i.e. equal time to each, or transparency if not; rooms and environment; materials for the unengaged participant (both relevant and irrelevant);
- the use of a flip chart or some transportable document.

Maintaining separate confidences – caucusing

The civil mediator holds secrets so as to build a picture of a realistically achievable outcome and to encourage discussion about sensitive issues and options in a confidential environment – 'caucusing'. Can family mediators ever maintain separate confidences without appearing to collude? There would need to be a new agreement to mediate to do so. Would this only be in finance and property matters? And before family mediators again consider rejecting this as anathema to their art, why is it so successful in civil mediation, and would it not at least be appropriate in hybrid cases?

Shuttling at a distance

Once one acknowledges the possibility that family or hybrid mediations need not be face to face, how far can one go in time and space? In cases of serious violence where a common interest remains in making arrangements for children or resolving finances, the shuttle could be within the same building, but on different days. And where the difficulties are of distance, why should mediation not be in different places, using various means of communication from video link to managed telephone ('tele-mediation') or online communication? The latter could range from simple email to model communication to a sophisticated online dispute resolution (ODR) package, to interaction in a virtual world. Acknowledging that the ongoing-relationship-based nature of family mediation will usually require a face-to-face component, there must be cases where an ability to offer other modes of communication will provide a satisfactory alternative to litigation.

6.3.7 Incorporating insights from collaborative family law (CFL) into the hybrid model

The role of the family consultant (often a mediator) in collaborative law is discussed elsewhere (see **Chapter 5**) and the development of CFL has much to teach mediators. What for example about the greater forensic quality of CFL? Would this challenge the impartiality of the mediator? Or the greater preparedness to bring in third-party experts such as accountants and barristers?

But if every separating couple with outstanding issues about children and finance lies at a unique point on the continuum between emotional/relationship transformation and commercial bargain, between therapeutic/facilitative and law-based resolution, is not the optimum model for family ADR one where the specialist mediator becomes the manager of a discrete process in which the lawyers are always potentially contributing actively, in a unique model that draws on the best of not only the civil and family mediation processes but also CFL, all of which might prove inadequate on their own? It could be argued that only mediation, and particularly the model of co-mediation that combines the specialist family lawyer and family therapist, provides the robustness and flexibility to enable this. That is, the complexity and entrenchment described above is best managed by the mediator, calling in partisan lawyers in a sort of upside-down CFL or collaborative mediation. Could this be the starting point for any alternative to litigation?

In this dynamic way, civil and family mediation and CFL can inform each other's practices. But what of the wider relationship between lawyers and mediators?

6.4 MEDIATORS AND LAWYERS WORKING IN PARTNERSHIP

> Partnership and cooperation is not a choice; it is the only way to advance our common humanity. (Barack Obama, Berlin, 24 July 2008)

6.4.1 Transformations

Those of us who mediate in disputes already deeply entrenched in litigation will recognise the transformation which we aspire to effect for clients and their families, from entrenched, adversarial, self-interested, in a vacuum or with a silo mentality and focused on fighting the battle, to cooperative, collaborative, engaged in effective communication and dialogue, focused on working towards a common solution, and on parenting or working in partnership. But what if there were a similar transformation also for us as practitioners?

This would create a paradigm shift in our working practice, towards a model of ADR that is truly multidisciplinary and collaborative. Our capacity to assist in the resolution of the complex and entrenched cases that elude us when we work alone would be substantially enhanced.

6.4.2 Why is it important to work together?

There are a number of reasons for this:

1. We are failing to meet the needs of those who wish to resolve all property, finance and children matters through all-issues mediation (AIM).
2. There is a gap between the court-based ancillary relief dispute resolution process and other ADR.
3. As family lawyers and mediators we have a shared ethical base and mutual interest in better outcomes for families.
4. It is cost effective for clients.
5. We need to provide a real process choice to clients – as shown in the leaflet, *Divorce and Separation: Choosing the Right Process for You* (Resolution, 2009).

6.4.3 Stimulating mutual confidence and understanding

Lawyers' and mediators' trust and experience of each other is patchy. So the solution will also be multifaceted, just like the tackling of embedded communication difficulties between clients. It will include local seminars and training, shared experience of working methods and the better use of existing structures such as local family justice councils (LFJCs), CFL practice and organisational development groups (PODs), mediation consortia or Resolution groups.

A code of practice or good practice guide encouraging the support of fellow professionals, much as Resolution has developed in relation to *opposing* lawyers, might help. But essentially it will only be achieved by collaborative, multidisciplinary organisations working on a local scale and in individual cases.

6.4.4 Developing the interdisciplinary model: some principles

Lawyers need to be encouraged to invest in the process in which their clients are engaged. Change is required on both sides. Lawyers are too often excluded by mediators in the name of purity of the process. Mediators need to be demonstrating active support for the lawyer/client relationship.

We should see the ADR process as one that is not confined to the mediation room, but rather a comprehensive interdisciplinary process like that of the court, that has a number of interlocking and different facets but, unlike the court, is infinitely variable in terms of pace, components and outcome.

Expanding the model both vertically and horizontally in this way risks compromising the basic principles of impartiality, confidentiality and particularly client ownership. For this reason, the terms of the collaborative work must be made explicit and negotiated by all at the outset. The parameters of the professional relationship and the extent to which information is to be shared, understandings about the availability of court orders and other materials, timescales and any compromise to privilege need to be scrupulously articulated.

If lawyers remain involved, why bother with the mediator? Because the non-partisan mediator provides the impartial arena – the best opportunity for a cooperative outcome; and where the model is expanded, that role becomes even more important. Chapter 16 of H. Brown, B. McHugh and N. Dawson, *Managing Difficult Divorce Relationships* (Resolution, 2006) provides persuasive guidance and models.

6.4.5 Lawyers' indirect involvement in the mediation process

The greatest complaint of solicitors is that they are left out of the loop. To address this, many services now routinely copy all materials to solicitors unless asked not to and use detailed letters or interim summaries with clear exposition of the difficulties and how they might be overcome cooperatively, or what advice about best and worst alternatives to negotiated agreement/costs estimate the lawyer might offer at this stage. Typically, at the interim summary stage mediators set out the process options available to clients, including a discussion with their solicitors as to whether it would be cost effective for them to become actively involved.

It is vital to mirror the contact with solicitors. There is no substitute for balanced correspondence recording all that has been discussed, and copied to the clients. Online communications are another way of cost-effectively and transparently working together at a common problem. Finally, if mediators can demonstrate support for the client/lawyer relationship, they are much more likely to get reciprocal assistance.

6.4.6 The myth of the information/advice divide

A frequent area of difficulty is the extent to which lawyers feel mediators go too far or not far enough in giving legal guidance. We may identify four layers of legal guidance:

1. Guiding principles from statute or case law, e.g. the welfare of the child is paramount or 'fairness is the guiding principle'.
2. Checklists of commonsense guidelines, e.g. the welfare checklist, or considerations under s.25 of the Matrimonial Causes Act 1973.
3. Guidance from case law, e.g. *Stack* v. *Dowden* [2007] UKHL 17, [2007] 1 FLR 1858, the greater acceptance of shared residence, or the *Payne* v. *Payne* [2001] EWCA Civ 166, [2001] 1 FLR 1052 principles.
4. Guidance from understanding of local circumstances, e.g. CAFCASS resources and procedures, judicial approach to clean break or nominal spousal maintenance, or the effectiveness of the local financial dispute resolution (FDR) appointment.

The further into these layers the mediator and clients can go, the more informed their options exploration will be, and the more robust the ADR process, particularly if conducted *in the shadow of the law*. So the quality, standard and depth of knowledge of the family mediator should be no less than that of any other family justice practitioner. It is the function, role and environment that differ in the distinction between information/guidance and advice, not the depth of knowledge, whether one works in a partisan or an impartial role. The mediator needs this knowledge and experience to set parameters for exploring options and finding common ground; the lawyer needs it, for example, to explore ambiguity to get the best for the individual client. Whereas s.25 of the Matrimonial Causes Act 1973 has become uncertain and unsatisfactory for lawyers and judges, for those in mediation this uncertainty simply opens up options and opportunities.

6.4.7 Direct involvement in the mediation room

There is scope for considerable flexibility as to how and when lawyers might be introduced into the mediation room. The aims of direct involvement might include giving advice alongside the process, testing reality, concluding a binding agreement, clarifying controversial disclosure issues (e.g. family companies) or redressing imbalance. As to subject matter, the model is likely to suit finance or AIM cases with a degree of complexity or entrenchment, including TOLATA 1996 and hybrid cases, or where ancillary proceedings and children issues have become enmeshed.

As to model, a conscious attempt to replicate the FDR, at an earlier stage, at a fraction of the cost and substituting the judge's discretion with the clients' control, can be particularly effective. Otherwise, the model is infinitely flexible as to number and length of sessions, participants and format. It is clear that some lawyer mediators are more comfortable with simply adapting the civil model into a shuttled settlement meeting. Others assume that the lawyers will remain in the room with their clients. But as long as the purpose defines the process, and the process is transparently negotiated and follows first principles, any modification may be appropriate.

The day will come when lawyers see referral to a mediator as trusted collaborator just as the instruction of counsel, independent financial adviser or other jointly appointed expert.

6.5 THE IMPLICATIONS OF PRIVATE LAW CHILDREN ACT PROCEEDINGS FOR MEDIATION MODELS

6.5.1 The need for integration and the challenge to integrity

Mediation is becoming far more integrated into private Children Act proceedings. It is vital that its integrity and dynamic development must not be diluted to meet the resource needs of the Private Law Programme, Ministry of Justice (MoJ) and Legal Services Commission (LSC). This is all about boundaries and models, communication and partnerships, rules, genius and art – and on it depends the success or failure of any new government initiative to develop mediation usage.

The linear model that assumes mediation breaks down, proceedings begin, and mediation is never tried again is inadequate. In many cases, the mediator, potentially as process-manager, may want to encourage the parties both to protect their positions by starting proceedings and to continue mediation to develop communication and militate against the worst adversarial impact of the proceedings.

After proceedings are instituted, there is a growing awareness that mediation may be particularly valuable. Its basic principles transform the environment of the conflict into one capable of producing more long-term positive outcomes. And yet it is those principles that again are most under threat when mediation is conducted alongside the proceedings. A balance needs to be struck between maintaining those principles and moving to a next generation of mediation models that no longer exist in a vacuum but rather are in dialogue with, and informed by, the litigation. So, whilst mediation should remain a universe complete unto itself, posited on a different theoretical and ethical model of resolution from the adversarial family justice system, we must not miss opportunities to develop a robust ADR process informed by and informing the exercise of the court's authority.

6.5.2 Expectations of the court and principles of mediation: the mediator as juggler

> The court orders the parties to attend voluntary mediation. (A recent order)

Very often, the court may have different expectations of the mediation process, sometimes because of an inadequate understanding. (A model for improving that understanding are the multidisciplinary ADR subcommittees of the London Family Justice Council.) The solution will lie in a balancing of the needs of the litigation process with the four basic principles of mediation.

In terms of impartiality, mediators use parenting plans and readily accept that, as part of a definition of impartiality or neutrality, mediators have a special concern for children. The Midland judges' statement of expectations (**www.judiciary.gov.uk**), the LSC Funding Code trigger (**www.legalservices.gov.uk/civil/guidance/funding_code.asp**), and Form C100 also put glosses on both the voluntariness of the process and the impartiality of the mediator which need to be transparently articulated.

As for voluntariness itself, mediation must remain a voluntary process. For it not to be would infringe LSC and lead family mediation body codes of practice. It could not be funded in the same way. A mediator might well want to keep in mind the extent to which clients are really volunteering to participate in any particular mediation. To take a recent example, directed mediation assessment as contact activity clearly challenges the mediator to hold to the integrity of the model without wasting the opportunity to introduce something new into the litigation process.

And as for client control, parents must be enabled to regain some control over their decision taking whilst in the midst of proceedings.

So we may need to move to a less absolute, more explicitly graduated, set of principles, the development of privilege being a good example.

6.5.3 A more sophisticated model of modified privilege

The President's Revised Family Law Programme, effective from 1 April 2010 but intended to come 'fully into effect' by 4 October 2010, assumes there will be cases where informed consent should be given to the waiving of privilege to inform both the mediator and the court. Mediation bodies have responded by welcoming the opportunities this enhanced cooperation provides, but also warning of the dangers this presents to voluntary, impartial, confidential mediation. The solution may lie in the development of a more sophisticated approach to privilege, provided this is appropriately supported and supervised.

Whether mediation is attempted pre-proceedings or subsequently, and provided clients give informed consent, it will often be in their interests for the courts to have some understanding of at least the outcome of the process, since this will avoid duplication and misunderstanding.

It may be possible to separate the privilege that applies to different strands of the mediation subject matter (always assuming that mediation privilege is absolute, a matter that has already become controversial in the civil field). Consideration might be given to sharing some or all of the following:

- safeguarding information;
- bare information about whether the parties attended the mediation assessment meeting;
- shared information about children's welfare, family structure, factual issues (see the open financial statement);
- bare information about agreement reached;
- detailed proposals;
- mediators' evaluative comments or reflections; and
- children's wishes and feelings.

It might be dangerous to allow this modification of privilege to develop on a case-by-case basis. There would at the least need to be some modification of the agreement to mediate. However it should be possible to negotiate a clear agreement, subject to legal advice, to partially waive the privilege – the clients thereby retaining control and ownership but providing the information required for cooperation and partnership.

A memorandum of understanding might therefore include the following:

> A and B propose, subject to legal advice, that the privilege that attaches to this Summary may be lifted to the extent that it may be disclosed to CAFCASS or the courts.

6.5.4 Could mediation ever not be voluntary or privileged?

There will be occasions when we modify the mediation model so far that it cannot be called mediation as understood by lead body codes of practice. One example would be *med-arb*; another might be an *expert* model of assessment as to the capacity of parents to work together, e.g. court-directed appropriate dispute resolution (CDADR). The main features of this are:

- It uses the mediation service as a jointly appointed expert.
- There is a definitive assessment of the parents' ability to cooperate.
- Court documents are available within the mediation process.
- The mediator reports to the court.
- It is not fully voluntary, impartial or confidential, but gives the client a sense of ownership by explicitly articulated additional ground rules, e.g. looking at what can be agreed, not what is in dispute; working cooperatively at solving the problem, not fighting the adversarial battle; looking forward positively, not looking backward judgementally.

(For more on this, see Neil Robinson, 'A New Model of Court Directed Mediation', [2006] Fam Law 139.)

6.6 GENERAL IMPLICATIONS

If the development of models is to move beyond individual creativity, into more widespread acceptance, at some point there will need to be:

- spaces for interdisciplinary dialogue, such as collaborative/mediator practice groups and LFJC ADR committees;
- advanced training, preferably on a multidisciplinary basis;
- conversion of individual modifications into formal guidance and good practice;
- new materials, such as modified agreements to mediate;
- a code of practice for interdisciplinary working, like the Resolution code of practice;
- consideration of a coherent public funding regime that incentivises all forms of ADR.

CHAPTER 7

Assembling the dispute resolution team

Juliet Felton, Margaret Kelly and Karen Ritchie

7.1 WHY TEAMS?

It is now widely recognised that the break up of a relationship is not only a legal matter requiring the expertise of lawyers, but a life changing time in many other ways and input from other professionals in other disciplines is extremely important.

7.1.2 Involving other professions

Other professionals can help drive the dispute resolution process forward or assist with an impasse. This is usually much easier to achieve when they have been introduced early in the process. Where this is not the case it is not uncommon for clients to be resistant to taking advice from unfamiliar professionals coming, as they see it, unexpectedly from outside the close relationships they have with their lawyer or mediator.

The possibility of involving other professionals should be raised with clients early on in the collaborative family law process to avoid creating a perception that the involvement of these professionals somehow represents a problem or failure on the part of the client, or questioning why their lawyer cannot deal with the issues arising.

7.2 MEMBERS OF THE TEAMS AND THEIR ROLES

7.2.1 The lawyer

The collaborative lawyer

A collaborative lawyer must be a member of Resolution and have practised family law for a minimum period of three years post-qualification. Resolution has set out rules for unqualified practitioners to train and these can be found on the Resolution website (**www.resolution.org.uk**).

TRAINING

Collaborative law training is organised by Resolution. The foundation course is three days long. At the end of the course the lawyer is able to take on collaborative law cases.

CPD

Collaborative lawyers must obtain at least six hours of Resolution-approved CPD training in each year of membership excluding the first year.

PODS

Collaborative lawyers belong to practice and organisational development groups (PODs). These are groups of collaborative professionals who meet periodically to discuss collaborative issues and cases. A collaborative lawyer must attend a minimum of four meetings each year.

ROLE

The collaborative lawyer will provide their client with legal advice, liaise with the collaborative lawyer for the other party, and attend four-way meetings. Between meetings the lawyers will speak to each other to agree agendas for meetings, identify any hotspots and try to avoid a situation where rabbits are drawn from hats.

The collaborative lawyers will also, together with the clients, explore the possibility of instructing other professionals. If it is decided to use other professionals, the collaborative lawyers will generally identify and instruct them. Together with clients they will agree what, if any, part they will play in four-way meetings.

The lawyer mediator

Barristers, solicitors and other legal professionals may train as mediators. They will need to complete mediation training and may practise the joint mediation model, the sole mediation model, or both. Training is provided by a number of bodies including Resolution.

Normally lawyer mediators are trained to deal with 'all issues mediation' (matters involving both financial issues and children issues). A mediator may be instructed in a matter that is proceeding in the collaborative model, to assist on a particular issue or a range of issues depending on the needs of the case.

Mediators do not give advice to either couple; rather they facilitate discussion and explore possibilities with a view to helping the couple reach an agreement that is acceptable to both of them. The mediators may consider it appropriate to involve other professionals and will discuss this with the parties in the mediation sessions.

Joint mediation

Here there are two mediators: one is a trained lawyer, the other is a family mediator. The mediators will attend all sessions together. The responsibility for work to be done between sessions will be agreed between the mediators.

Sole mediation

A lawyer mediator or family mediator trained in sole mediation can undertake mediation without the assistance of another mediator. Many trained in sole mediation also practise joint mediation as cases can benefit from the input of the two disciplines.

The lawyer advising during the mediation process

As the mediators do not provide legal advice the parties will normally have solicitors advising them in parallel to the mediation process. That solicitor does not need to be trained in mediation.

7.2.2 Counsel

Barristers may be trained as collaborative law practitioners or as mediators and in that role the information regarding collaborative lawyers and lawyer mediators above is relevant (see **7.2.1**).

During the course of mediation or the collaborative process the parties may agree that an opinion from counsel would help to resolve an issue that is sticking. It should be made clear to counsel that the piece of work is being sought in the context of mediation or collaborative law.

7.2.3 Counsel trained in collaborative family law

There are now a number of barristers who have trained in collaborative family law – with solicitors in the collaborative law foundation training courses which have been running now for several years; more recently, Resolution has run a training course tailor-made for barristers. The idea is that counsel will be used as joint experts in the collaborative process if a difficult issue arises. Alternatively, counsel could be used as additional members of the team on both sides in order to resolve trickier collaborative cases.

Although counsel currently have been granted direct access in collaborative law cases, it is widely agreed they will not use that facility and that their preference will be to receive their instructions via solicitors, rather than being clients' direct legal representatives. It is hoped that practitioners will now consider the use of counsel more readily in collaborative law cases and hopefully the team ethos will continue to grow.

7.2.4 The independent financial adviser (IFA)

Independence

Note 1 of the guidance to rule 19 of the Solicitors' Code of Conduct 2007 states that 'independence is a core duty'. Hence any financial adviser involved in the CDR process must be able to offer whole-of-market advice rather than the products of just one provider.

An IFA involved in a CDR process should have sufficient experience in dealing with this type of case work. They should be empathetic and able to explain financial concepts to clients who may struggle with finances or who have never dealt with them previously.

Resolution accredited IFAs

It is worth noting that there is currently no traditional qualification held by IFAs that covers any aspect of divorce or separation. In response to this Resolution launched an accreditation scheme for IFAs specialising in family law financial planning. A current list of IFAs who have successfully become accredited can be found on the members' website under affiliate members. They have an additional logo. Although Resolution cannot insist that members only use accredited IFAs the list of advisers is a resource available to members.

For IFAs who may be interested in becoming accredited specialists, a prospectus detailing entry criteria and procedures is available from Resolution.

When can an IFA be used in a collaborative family law team?

IFAs can be involved in mediation, collaborative or round-table processes. The remit of their work needs to be agreed at the outset to ensure the process is not compromised at any point. For instance, is the IFA being enlisted as a joint expert to advise on one particular issue (e.g. pensions), as a true financial neutral or to assist one party only in terms of education and understanding?

IFAs will actively look for guidance on their level of involvement and work required. Where possible they should also be asked for an estimate of their fees in advance and clients' agreement sought as to the method of payment.

It can be beneficial if the first meeting between the client(s) and the IFA takes place with the collaborative family lawyer or mediator present. This allows the lawyer to brief the IFA in front of the clients and the IFA to explain in more detail how they fit into the process and what value they can add.

During the meeting the IFA should:

(a) address any concerns regarding their role raised by the client(s);
(b) agree work and timescales;

(c) highlight potential problems;
(d) provide details of their hourly rate and a fee estimate.

Types of work that an IFA can undertake and the benefits to the CDR team

The earlier an IFA is brought into the process the more benefit can be achieved. This includes the following:

1. **Assistance with disclosure and information gathering.** If the IFA does this at the outset they can request additional information that may be of benefit and save time later in the process. For instance, they can obtain surrender quotations on endowments and request information on pensions to ascertain options to discuss with the clients. Of course the IFA can be brought in later to address these additional areas but if information has not been requested or is missing it can slow the process down and cost the client more money as more information requests are sent.
2. **Budgeting.** This is an area that many clients struggle with, especially if they have not been involved in the day-to-day reality of the household budget. IFAs can assist by working through expenditure questionnaires. This is particularly helpful when done with both clients as each may have dealt with a different area of the family finances and be able to share their experience of costs.
3. **Cash flow planning and settlement option modelling.** This can be particularly useful in an impasse where both parties can be shown the effect of their proposals on each other's financial future as a cash flow graph. This can also be used to consider the effect of different options, for instance pension sharing over a cash lump sum, or future cash payouts from business sales. This type of planning can also be used to work out the minimum lump sum a party may need to maintain their lifestyle over the rest of their lives.
4. **Specific technical work, e.g. pensions.** IFAs are often brought in to deal with specific questions on pensions. An actuary may also be needed in some cases to assist with the calculations but an IFA can help explain the options and their implications to clients. The IFA can also help educate a client who may have little understanding of pensions.

IFA issues specific to collaborative law practice

An IFA brought into the collaborative process is known as a financial neutral, i.e. with no particular affiliation to either client. When acting as a neutral in a collaborative law case an IFA must comply with the following criteria:

1. They will be paid fees, based on an hourly rate or a pre-agreed fixed fee.
2. They will not make specific product recommendations (i.e. not recommend any particular product in such a way as to fall within the Financial Services

Authority's definition of regulated advice). Their role is to provide a mix of information and education to the collaborative process that allows the clients to deal with the transition, develop their own financial solution and move on with an understanding of their future economic circumstances.
3. They will not implement any financial strategies for either client. They will provide a full briefing to an IFA acting as implementer to ensure the implementation is handled quickly and efficiently.
4. They will not accept commissions or referral fees from other IFAs who may later implement financial strategies for either spouse.
5. Should the collaborative process break down, the IFA may not be retained by either spouse (unless the collaborative agreement requires their involvement as a neutral at a given date in the future).

Compliance with these criteria means:

1. The impartiality of the IFA acting as a neutral cannot be challenged.
2. The absence of specific product recommendations ensures that the settlement is not influenced by the need to generate commission.
3. A neutral who assists in the financial settlement can be re-engaged later in the collaborative process if required by a change in the couple's circumstances – if the IFA has taken on one of the couple as an ongoing client then their duty of care will preclude them from later acting as a neutral in the same case.
4. The IFA's motivation is the same as the collaborative lawyers' in seeking a positive collaborative outcome, because none of them can work for either client if the process breaks down.

Why is neutrality so important?

In the collaborative process, the IFA as financial neutral moves away from their traditional role of expert supplying a technical, objective analysis. Instead, they have to tailor their work to take into account the emotions that may surround the assets accumulated during a marriage.

So rather than tell a client that they cannot have what they want, their role is to allow the couple to voice their concerns and emotions with the ultimate aim of allowing them to reflect on the financial reality of their position and come to their own conclusions regarding the financial implications of life after divorce.

Reframing and reflecting on this reality may be more effective than giving specific advice about a final outcome. This allows the IFA to facilitate a solution and agreement without appearing to have created it. The end result should be an agreement that stands the test of time.

The couple's decision to enter the collaborative process and engage a financial neutral should ensure that they enter that process with a level of trust and a greater willingness for cooperation. If the IFA does not adhere to the strict requirements of neutrality there is a substantial risk that one of the parties will perceive they are not being treated equally and that their emotions have not been acknowledged. The subsequent breakdown of trust in the IFA reduces the chances of successful resolution.

Collaborative training for IFAs and other professionals

Skills training is now available to both IFAs and other professionals such as accountants, actuaries, surveyors, etc. It is a two-day course focusing on the collaborative process and how it works, the professional's involvement in the process, and role plays with existing collaboratively trained lawyers. Further details are available from Resolution.

Payments for introducing clients to IFAs

If the IFA is acting as a neutral in a collaborative case they should under no circumstances pay an introducer's fee or commission to the introducing lawyer.

The Solicitors Regulation Authority (SRA) currently requires law firms to inform clients about any commissions they receive. Recent announcements from the SRA indicate that firms will soon have to demonstrate why retaining that money is in the client's best interests.

7.2.5 Accountants/valuers/actuaries

Experts in these fields will be called in to all types of dispute resolution process as and when necessary, e.g. where a valuation of a business property is required, or advice on how to split a pension to achieve a particular result is sought. For the collaborative process, Resolution now runs a familiarisation training course specifically for these experts, which provides them with some insight into how collaborative practice differs from traditional practice and to experience role play of the collaborative process. Collaborative lawyers are instructing these experts with increasing frequency as part of the team approach.

When instructing an expert, care should be taken to be clear as the report may be used in court proceedings if the collaborative process breaks down. It may also be useful for one of the team to speak to the expert first to make sure they have the correct expertise and to flag up what you are asking them to report on.

7.2.6 The family consultant (or divorce coach)

There are two parts to divorce: the legal and the emotional. The legal part is dealt with by lawyers and family consultants can assist in the emotional aspects. In the same way that financial experts can be called into all forms of dispute resolution, so the family consultant can be of enormous help within these processes too.

In England and Wales the term 'family consultant' is used instead of 'divorce coach' (United States), but for some the terms are interchangeable.

Family consultants within the collaborative process provide short-term support for the emotional and psychological aspects that arise during separation and divorce. They work with individuals, couples and families to help those concerned to maintain or develop healthy communication, provide insight and look for solution-based outcomes.

Prior qualifications, training and experience

To comply with Resolution requirements, family consultants must be educated to degree level and have recognised professional qualifications or a licence allowing practice, in at least one of the following disciplines:

- psychology;
- social work;
- marriage and family therapy;
- clinical counselling;
- mediation (with Family Mediators' Association, National Family Mediation of England or Resolution accreditation).

They should be a member in good standing with the relevant professional organisation that regulates their practice, as it is this body that will regulate their practice as a family consultant. They must have three years' post-qualification experience related to couples and family work, and they must have documented insurance coverage for their professional practice.

In addition to the above, family consultants will have, or be willing to gain through additional training, a comprehensive understanding of at least two of the following:

- mediation and collaborative law;
- child development;
- family systems theory;
- dynamics of separation and divorce;
- the basic workings of the family court system and legal process for their jurisdiction;
- facilitating multi-party meetings/family conferencing and managing the respective communications.

They must have attended and completed approved family consultant familiarisation training; provide documentation, on demand, of current enhanced level police clearance; be in supervised practice and provide a reference from their supervisor; and actively participate in their local POD, attending a minimum of four POD meetings per year.

Any family consultant working as a child consultant, or having any contact with children, will have completed appropriate specialised training and, as above, hold current enhanced level police clearance, Criminal Records Bureau (CRB) check.

What do family consultants do?

As part of the collaborative law process family consultants are there to help couples, individuals and families navigate the emotional aspects of separation and divorce. They help couples and families to manage any difficulties that may derail or delay the collaborative law process. They can deal with individual issues as they arise and help the couple to find a workable, positive and agreed outcome and this in turn will support the legal team to do their job more smoothly. They attend the four-way meeting if requested by an individual or a couple. Family consultants should make it clear that the work they undertake is limited to short-term, targeted intervention aimed at supporting the parties during the collaborative process and/or supporting them during the process of separation, divorce and the establishment or continuation of cooperative parenting.

How do they help couples?

Family consultants can:

- identify and help clients to resolve disputes and lower the emotional temperature of the process;
- support clients by understanding difficult issues and unresolved differences;
- give couples a place to explore any concerns and fears of separation and divorce (and beyond) regarding parenting;
- create an environment where it is safe for individuals or couples to vent difficult emotions;
- develop and improve healthy communication and therefore help the ongoing four-way process meetings;
- assist with, and inform the lawyers of, difficult issues as agreed and discussed with clients as they arise;
- develop coping strategies for couples and families setting short-, medium- and long-term goals;
- assist couples to explore parenting through divorce and co-parenting skills;
- develop a parenting plan and discuss different or same-style parenting and issues that may arise;

- invite clients to understand their path that led them to separate and acknowledge their co-creation of this outcome whilst still respecting each other as individuals.

Family consultants can work with individuals, couples or entire families. If appropriate they may also work with the client's partners. Though the work is time limited it is also sometimes appropriate to build in review sessions at the client's request. These can be agreed as a 'health check' after the divorce process is over and the clients have separated. It is the aftercare support which may help clients to resolve difficulties or to revisit and adjust agreements if they seem not to be working (i.e. parenting plans).

Risk assessment

It is the duty of the family consultant to make it known to their clients that they have a responsibility to report any concerns regarding the possibility of harm to self or others, including child protection issues. Family consultants need to encourage a couple or individual to self-disclose any concerns to the appropriate authority, be it police, social services or their doctor.

If they fail to do this then the family consultant needs to inform them that they are legally bound to report them to one of the appropriate authorities. A version of this may also be included in the family consultant's professional body's code of ethics. Couples should be aware of the family consultant's code of ethics at the start of their work together.

Referrals

Referrals can be done as follows:

- self-referral;
- referral by a lawyer;
- referral by another professionals (i.e. doctor, psychiatrist, therapist);
- through the courts.

7.3 ADDITIONAL SUPPORT OR THERAPY

It may be beneficial for an individual who needs further support for deeper issues or longer-term intervention to be referred to a psychotherapist or counsellor. The family consultant may suggest this whilst working with a couple if they feel that the client would benefit from further individual support. This can be arranged by a client's doctor or by the client using the British Association for Counselling and Psychotherapy (BACP) or United Kingdom Council for Psychotherapy (UKCP) websites and self-referring. Referral can also be suggested by the family consultant to the client.

7.4 CHILDREN'S NEEDS

Children will nearly always react in some way to parents separating. Some children may need to talk to an impartial third party regarding what is happening within their family. It is not uncommon for divorcing couples to discuss their relationship openly in front of their children either with friends, family members, or others. This can be extremely damaging to children and should be avoided at all times.

Tolerance and allowance must be given for children to adjust. It is worth bearing in mind the following:

1. Children need to voice their own concerns, fears and feelings about their parents' separation and divorce.
2. It is important for children to maintain a strong relationship with both parents unless there are concerns regarding the child's safety.
3. Children who show mild behavioural disturbances as the separation and divorce process continues may settle as the parents adjust to their new separate lives. Observation of their children and monitoring of behaviour by the parents is important at this stage. It may be informative and useful in drawing up parenting plans and discussing parenting styles. The parents will, at some point, be going through the change to parenting from two homes with different styles of parenting, social grouping and new partners. Children will almost always have a reaction whilst they adjust.
4. A family consultant will need to be aware of any child behavioural issues and discuss any concerns that arise regarding children first the parents. If the family consultant has concerns about what they are being told by the parents they can suggest that the parents get additional advice and help.
5. Children who are showing signs of distress may be exhibiting extreme and difficult behaviour, truanting from school, physical harm to self or others, the use of recreational drugs, alcohol abuse or taking part in illegal activities. The parents should inform their lawyers, family doctor and seek professional help with additional support from the family consultant.
6. Children need to be given information about their parents' separation using age-appropriate language. Children should never be told lies or half-truths as this does long-term damage. Parents may need to refer back to the family consultant for information and *how to do* skills in tackling conversations with children.

There are psychiatrists, psychologists, psychotherapists and counsellors with training in child development and family systems who specialise in working with children. This work may also be carried out by the family consultant.

7.5 FLEXIBILITY OF PROCESS

Unlike the court process, neither mediation nor collaborative law are processes where one size fits all; rather, they are tailor-made to fit each case. There is, therefore, no prescriptive way to run a matter, subject to keeping within the rules of the process.

As we have seen, a mediator or counsel may be enlisted to assist in a collaborative case, as may any of the other experts listed above. The team will evolve and people will come in and out as the case proceeds. The assistance of other professionals will always be sought following an agreement reached between the parties.

7.6 COORDINATION OF A TEAM

In the UK one of the collaborative lawyers normally coordinates the team. Where the members of the team are instructed by one party only (e.g. family consultant) then the solicitor representing that party will usually coordinate them.

In the United States the financial neutral or a mental health professional often takes on the role of team coordinator. There is no reason why this should not happen in the UK and this is something that could be developed as practitioners become more experienced.

In mediation, joint mediators will coordinate any professionals they enlist to the team with the joint mediators agreeing who will do what.

In a sole mediation the sole mediator will have the task of coordinating the team.

7.7 COMMUNICATION BETWEEN THE TEAM MEMBERS

Communication between the members of the team is the key to success, particularly in collaborative practice. Keeping all parties involved via regular communication reaps rewards in ensuring the whole team is up to date and able to make timely suggestions.

Meetings between collaborative team members can be prohibitively costly or difficult if members of the team are separated by large distances. Equally teleconferences can be difficult to arrange due to court commitments or other client work, etc. often resulting in delays for the clients. One option now used by some collaborative practitioners is setting aside one morning per week to be available for collaborative conferences. How best to deal with this is something that can be discussed within PODs.

Individual PODs could consider the form and timeliness of communication between the professions and who requires what and when. Thought should be given as to the form and amount of written communication, specifically emails.

Debrief meetings between the various professionals, following the conclusion of a case, are invaluable.

7.8 NEUTRALITY OF TEAM MEMBERS IN COLLABORATIVE PRACTICE

The concept of neutrality may apply to any of the professions involved in a neutral role.

Resolution has adopted the International Academy of Collaborative Professionals (IACP) Ethical Standards for Collaborative Practitioners and these state:

> A collaborative practitioner who serves on a collaborative case in a neutral role shall adhere to that role, and shall not engage in any continuing client relationship that would compromise the collaborative practitioner's neutrality. Working with either or both client(s) or with their child(ren) outside of the collaborative process is inconsistent with that neutral role.
>
> A collaborative practitioner serving as a neutral financial specialist in a collaborative case shall not have an ongoing business relationship with a collaborative client during or after the completion of the collaborative case, but may assist the clients in completing the tasks specifically assigned to them by the clients' written, final agreement. Such assistance may not include the sale of financial products or other services.
>
> A collaborative practitioner serving as a child specialist may assist the family in divorce-related matters for the child(ren). Such assistance may not include becoming the child(ren)'s therapist.
>
> A collaborative practitioner serving as a neutral coach may assist the family in divorce-related matters. Such assistance may not include acting as a therapist for one or both parties.

CHAPTER 8

Funding

Angela Donen, Caroline Bowden, Margaret Kelly and Karen Ritchie

This chapter outlines some of the funding issues that arise in mediation and collaborative practice, including the availability of public funding, before exploring the options for payment available to privately funded clients.

8.1 MEDIATION

A mediator should always appear to be impartial and neutral. Nothing should disturb this principle. Mediation is a service for which payment is rightly expected. It is important that the payment does not interfere with the balance between the parties and the neutrality of the mediator.

A mediator should be sensitive where one person is paying for mediation and the other is not in case the paying party feels that the mediation is being spun out to incur maximum expense for the paying party. Equally, where a referral is made to mediation on behalf of a party who would be eligible for public funding it is important that their situation is not worsened because of the delay caused by mediation.

A mediator will be alert to a situation where one party is considerably better off than the other and yet the second party is not eligible for publicly funded mediation and finds the cost of mediation extremely burdensome.

When family mediation first started, public funding was not available. For the past decade public funding has been available and for the last eight years or so there has been a requirement that (in the majority of cases) a person who wants public funding to litigate a case must be referred for consideration as to its suitability for mediation. (Exemptions are provided on the CLS APP 7 form, some of which are certified by the client's solicitor and some are assessed by the mediator.) In publicly funded cases mediators must tell clients how much the likely costs of mediation will be and give an estimate of the cost of litigating.

Mediators are regulated by national bodies under the collective umbrella of the Family Mediation Council. Although each organisation may have originated in a different way, they all work to the same model and all work to the overarching regulations of the Family Mediation Council. There was a difference in funding by the Legal Services Commission of the not-for-profit sector (National Family Mediation) and the other mediators until October 2007, but since then all have been funded in exactly the same way.

8.1.1 Assessment

Most mediators have a system for assessing the suitability of a case for mediation whether or not it is publicly funded. In some cases this is called an induction, in others an assessment. Sometimes these assessments are conducted jointly with both parties present, and sometimes the parties attend separately.

During the assessment mediators consider:

(a) whether the parties understand the mediation agreement;
(b) the parties' eligibility for public funding;
(c) what the mediation is about;
(d) any issues which require special attention including (invariably) screening for domestic violence and child abuse.

For those individuals who are not eligible for public funding, the induction or assessment is free if the referral was made in order to assess suitability for mediation on behalf of a person who wishes to have public funding. Where public funding is not involved, some practices charge for the induction or assessment and some do not. It is worth checking.

8.1.2 Public funding

Publicly funded mediation is available at any time including prior to the issue of court proceedings, during court proceedings and after court proceedings.

If a case is suitable for mediation the mediator will continue to the first session either on the same occasion as assessment or on another occasion. The mediator is paid by the Legal Services Commission (LSC) for the assessment and receives a different payment depending on whether the case involves a child issue, a property and finance issue or where both issues are to be considered. The mediator is paid at a higher rate if the case moves beyond the first session whether or not there is an outcome. If an outcome statement or memorandum of understanding is provided then an additional payment is made but there is no additional payment for an open financial summary.

The property or money received as a result of mediation is exempt from the statutory charge. Where legal advice is provided in support of mediation under level 2 of the Family Help (Private) Fee Scheme this advice will also be exempt from the solicitor's charge if the case settles at this level and the case is not exceptional. The solicitor receives a bonus or settlement fee if the case settles at that level also.

8.1.3 Maximising resources

Mediation sometimes takes place when money is in short supply and it is essential that the time spent in mediation is limited. For example, in publicly funded cases there is a ceiling on what a mediation service will be paid regardless of the number of sessions involved or the amount of time spent. Where parties are not publicly funded but money is tight the number of sessions may need to be limited. For this reason it may be helpful to liaise with others who have been involved with the family to obtain information (solicitors, social services, etc.) and discover disclosure which has already taken place, correspondence which has been exchanged, etc.

Sometimes clients can be asked to do homework. For example, information can be obtained from clients in writing regarding what the issues for mediation are, what their particular priorities are, why they want those outcomes. They may be asked to consider what outcomes they think the other person may be looking for and why they think the other person will be looking for them. They can also be asked to consider three potential solutions for every given issue in mediation so that they do some of the thinking and option storming for themselves before they attend a session.

8.1.4 Third parties

During the course of a mediation it may be necessary to instruct third parties, e.g. a surveyor to value a home, a forensic accountant to value a business, or a psychologist to assess issues connected with risk of contact. There is very little flexibility under the public funding model for these payments to be met by the mediator. Where reports of this kind are needed the mediator, in appropriate circumstances, may refer back to the solicitors so that they can jointly instruct the expert whose report will become available within the mediation.

In the case of a privately funded mediation, with both parties' consent as to funding, the third party can be instructed by the parties through the mediator with full knowledge of both parties' solicitors. The essence of a single joint expert is that they are neutral and this neutrality can be emphasised if the mediator instructs them. Care should, however, be taken to establish whether the report will be within the confidentiality of the mediation or whether it will be open and available for use outside the mediation and the expert instructed should be clear about the extent of their involvement.

8.1.5 Cost of mediation

Each mediator will provide details of their own charges. Usually these will be available before the client makes a referral but if not, at the induction or assessment meeting. The mediation agreement will either contain details of costs or it will refer to a separate schedule detailing them. For the agreement to be binding it must make it clear who is to pay the charges so, e.g. it should have a default provision that if the parties do not agree that one of them will bear all of the charges, then they will bear them equally.

It is sometimes said that mediation is a cheaper option than court. It is certainly cheaper than a full court hearing. Mediation will not cut corners but it will cut out correspondence and phone calls because both parties are present during the mediation.

8.2 THE COLLABORATIVE PROCESS

In October 2009, following representations from Resolution, the Legal Services Commission proposed that collaborative law be added to the range of work available to family legal aid practitioners from 1 October 2010. Resolution worked hard to persuade the government to allow separating families eligible for legal aid to use collaborative law and welcomed this announcement as it means that more couples will able to avoid the acrimony of a full-blown court case – which in turn will help reduce the number of cases taking up expensive court time and will avoid stressful court delays.

However the level of payment for those collaboratively trained lawyers who are able to offer this option to their publicly funded clients is unsatisfactory as cases will only be remunerated at legal help level 2. Collaborative lawyers should note that use of family consultants and or other professionals within the process will not be possible. However, a referral to mediation could be made in tandem with the collaborative process for discrete issues such as concerns over children, parenting plans, etc. and this may go some way to addressing the specific needs of the parents and their children. Such mediators would of course need to be LSC competence assessed. Should collaborative clients need specialist help such as debt counselling, welfare benefits, housing, etc. clients can contact the relevant helpline for advice and may even obtain funding for further specialist advice from a lawyer if necessary. Each of these claims would be deemed to be separate and could be claimed for outside the collaborative process.

It will be possible from October 2010 to offer a collaborative divorce to clients not only where both are eligible for public funding but also where only one of them qualifies. Many cases where only one of the parties is eligible for public funding are currently dealt with successfully via mediation. These clients will now have another option to consider.

It is hoped that being able to offer the collaborative process to suitable publicly funded clients will assist in increasing the awareness of the process. Cases dealt with in this way will be monitored closely both by the LSC and by Resolution.

8.3 PRIVATE FUNDING

Clients who are not eligible for public funding must meet their own costs. Solicitors generally no longer wait until the end of a case for payment but require to be paid as the matter progresses.

Clients who find it difficult to meet legal and other associated fees from their day-to-day income may need to look at other ways of funding the process.

Before going down any route the clients should agree who will be responsible for any additional debts taken on, and how they will be dealt with in any asset schedules or if the process breaks down.

It is worth reminding clients that with any joint account that has an overdraft facility – or any joint loan – each party is responsible for all the debt run up on the account should the other person default.

Some funding options practitioners may wish to consider with their clients are outlined below.

8.3.1 Specialist funding for legal fees

There are several banks that provide litigation loans. At the moment the banks' security relies on court proceedings having been issued and the loans are therefore not available to parties in the collaborative process. This service may be available if the mediation process has started after proceedings are issued.

There are companies who offer funding facilities to solicitors. The firm of solicitors is a client of the company and a total amount available to the firm is agreed, at e.g. £500,000. It is then necessary for each client to complete a loan agreement. The client can draw down funds to meet bills. During the course of the proceedings the client pays interest, monthly, on the amount outstanding on the loan. At the end of the case or the expiration of a certain period of time the capital must be repaid. If the loan is not repaid or the client defaults, the solicitors' firm is responsible for the debt, although the company, working with the firm, will try to recover the debt from the client.

8.3.2 Borrowing

Remortgaging

If both clients are in agreement and have spare equity in the matrimonial home, or other property, they could approach their existing mortgage lender to see if they will increase the mortgage. In the short term this will increase the amount of monthly payments; in the long term it will increase the debts that will need to be paid off.

Mortgage holiday

Some mortgage lenders allow customers to take a mortgage holiday. However, the client must check the terms carefully and be aware that such a holiday will increase the outstanding balance, on which they will pay interest.

At the end of the holiday period the new monthly payments will be higher to reflect interest on the increased outstanding balance.

Interest-only mortgage

Clients could consider changing from a repayment to an interest-only mortgage to reduce monthly outgoings. Most lenders will allow this on payment of an administration fee.

Clients will need to bear in mind that the capital outstanding will never be paid off on an interest-only mortgage, so it should only be a short-term solution.

Bank loans

Bank loans are an expensive and inflexible form of debt. There are various search engines that clients can use to search for the best deal. The website **www.moneysavingexpert.com** provides useful information on the implications of taking out loans and credit cards.

Credit cards

Despite recent changes in credit availability there are zero per cent deals on credit card purchases available if the debt is to be repaid within a year. Longer credit deals are possible for higher interest rates. Again search engines offer a good starting point to explore the deal most suitable for the particular client.

8.3.3 Utilising investments

Clients could consider agreeing to withdraw lump sums or use regular income from their investments to fund the process. They should check with their accountant or financial adviser before going down this route as there may be tax implications.

8.3.4 Reducing day-to-day outgoings

This may seem like a tall order, particularly if the parties have recently started living separately but is worth exploring. A budgeting exercise could be useful in identifying costs that can be reduced, particularly in the short term, to free up cash to pay legal bills.

CHAPTER 9

Start-up

Kim Finnis

This chapter will look at the arrangements for preparing for and conducting the first mediation session and for starting out on the collaborative law process, to include the first four-way meeting. As these dispute resolution processes have differences they will be looked at separately. The preparation work will be considered first and then the arrangements for the first mediation session or four-way meeting.

Although a mediator may think of this stage as simply a practical one, they should be in no doubt that they have already stepped into the mediation arena. The mediator's ability to remain impartial and even-handed is essential at this stage, as is their skill in behaving in a balanced way in dealing with all the arrangements for the first session.

As is true of mediation, this initial stage in the collaborative law process does not just involve making sure that certain practical steps are in place. Although initially the parties will not have signed the participation agreement, the collaborative lawyer's abilities come into play from the outset. The work undertaken at this point is absolutely vital in laying the foundations that are necessary to ensure the process is an effective and constructive one for the parties.

This chapter will cover privately funded work. When publicly funded mediation is undertaken, various statutory and other procedural requirements will also have to be met to satisfy the Legal Services Commission's criteria. Following representations from Resolution, the government proposed in October 2009 that collaborative law be added to the range of work available to family legal aid practitioners from 1 October 2010.

9.1 PREPARING FOR THE FIRST MEDIATION SESSION

9.1.1 Sending out the necessary documents

Before the first mediation session both parties should be sent the following:

1. A preliminary information form.
2. A copy of the agreement to mediate.

3. Details of the mediator's charges and terms of business.
4. Confirmation of when and where the first mediation session will take place.
5. A map and directions.

The parties need to be advised that they must each complete their preliminary information form and return it to the mediator before the first mediation session, so that the mediator has time to consider it in advance.

In some cases the parties may also wish to be sent a mediation Form E to start to complete at this stage as this can be cost effective for them. In other cases, the parties may already have prepared Forms E before the first mediation session. If so, check to see if the parties want to send you copies before you meet. If there is any disagreement on how to proceed leave this issue for discussion at the first meeting. In all other cases mediation Forms E can be handed out at the first session.

If the mediation referral has come directly from solicitors it is helpful to write to them to acknowledge your instruction and confirm the date and time of the first mediation session.

9.1.2 Preliminary information forms

The preliminary information form provides the mediator with basic information about the parties and what they are looking to achieve in mediation. The mediator needs to read these forms carefully as they provide key information to help prepare for the first session. If either party has not returned their form in time, then the mediator will need to chase this up. This could be an indication of reluctance to attend, which is better addressed at this point, rather than be faced with non-attendance at the first meeting. The usual Resolution practice is for the mediator not to provide each party with a copy of the other's form. However, information from the forms can be shared by the mediator in general terms during the sessions. The preliminary information form is also a chance for the mediator to pick up on any anxieties the parties may have about meeting together, or concerns relating to domestic violence or abuse. If this arises the mediator should address these issues with the party in advance of the first session.

9.1.3 Agreement to mediate

The agreement to mediate sets out the ground rules for the mediation process and forms the bedrock of the entire mediation process. It deals with confidentiality, privilege, fees, practical matters and sets out the main aspects of the code of practice that the mediator subscribes to. The agreement to mediate indicates to the parties that the mediation process will be dealt with in a professional and business-like manner and avoids misunderstanding about the basis on which mediation is undertaken. Furthermore, it enables the parties to consider and confirm their commitment to mediation. Once signed, the agreement to mediate creates a written contract between the parties and the mediator. Should there be any disputes or subsequent court proceedings, reference will need to be made to the agreement to mediate. Resolution members can obtain a copy of the current agreement to mediate from the ADR committee's section of the Resolution website (**www.resolution.org.uk**). It is updated from time to time.

9.1.4 Dealing with questions

The parties may have questions at this point. At this stage the mediator should only deal with queries about the mediation procedure or initial arrangements and must make it clear that they will not discuss a party's views and position outside the mediation sessions. The mediator's role is to remain impartial, even-handed and behave in a balanced way. Any discussions the mediator has with the parties at this stage have to be handled sensitively and carefully.

9.1.5 Professional but informal ambiance: setting up your meeting room

The meeting room and reception arrangements need to be prepared with care. The environment created will assist in helping the couple feel at ease and in creating rapport. It is recommended to aim for a professional, but informal ambiance. Files and papers should be cleared. Ensure privacy and that you will not be disturbed. Arrange the chairs at suitable distance and angle for the parties to be comfortable. The use of a round table is probably the ideal. A table provides a place to put papers and write and also offers a barrier to help parties feel less vulnerable.

The following items need to be available in the meeting room for each session:

1. Flip chart and marker pens (avoid red pens; red is often associated with anger).
2. Box of tissues.
3. A calendar.
4. A calculator.
5. *At a Glance* (Family Law Bar Association/Class Legal).
6. Writing pads and pens (make sure these are identical) for the parties to use.
7. A jug of water and sufficient glasses (make sure glasses are identical).
8. Coffee/tea.

If the parties want to consider the arrangements for the children it will also be helpful to have to hand the parties' diaries and, depending on the children's ages, a copy of the children's school calendar(s).

The mediator needs to have the following documents available for the meeting:

1. Three copies of the agreement to mediate, for signature. One for each of the parties and one for themselves.
2. Two sets of the mediation Form E to hand to the parties, if they have not received these already.
3. Two sets of any other handouts that may provide useful information to the parties, e.g. with regard to: state benefits; divorce procedure; ancillary relief procedure; child support and parenting after parting.
4. If possible, where the parties have children, two copies of *Separation and Divorce: Helping Parents to Help Children* (Resolution).

9.1.6 Reception arrangements

Ensure that you are immediately notified as each party arrives in reception so that they are not left together for any length of time and not at all if there is any hostility. If needs be, arrange for separate waiting areas for the parties. The first to arrive could be shown into the meeting room straightaway, so the other party can then sit in reception. The mediator should do their best not to keep the parties waiting. This can be a very anxious time for them. Some mediators provide books and reading material in their reception or meeting rooms for the parties to browse whilst waiting, or borrow between sessions. (See **Appendix 2** for some suggestions.)

9.1.7 Co-mediation

The Resolution mediation model is a sole mediation one. If you are co-mediating, do make sure that your co-mediator is sent a copy of the preliminary information forms and you liaise direct with regard to the first session.

9.2 PREPARING TO START A COLLABORATIVE CASE

9.2.1 Preparing with your client – what are their objectives and goals?

Having established that the client wishes to use the collaborative law process to resolve matters, the first step is to explore with them why they have chosen this process, what their priorities are, what really matters to them and what are their goals and objectives from the process. The aim here is to help the client focus on their core values and interests, which ultimately will be expressed in the first four-way meeting and referred to throughout the collaborative process as their guiding objectives or *anchor statement*. This exploration with the client has been compared to peeling an onion. There are many layers involved once the client really starts to look at what is important to them. The collaborative lawyer might ask the client, 'What would the ideal outcome look like in say 18 months, and/or five years' time', or 'What do you want the process to enable you and your former spouse or partner to be able to do?' Initially, clients might mention they would like a reasonable home for themselves and their children, but in addition to this, they may also want to maintain a good working relationship with the other parent and/or for their children to have the benefit of close relations with both parents. During this discussion the collaborative lawyer can explain to their client that at the first four-way meeting they and their spouse or partner will be invited to express their objectives, so their former spouse or partner can hear them and they will be recorded so they can be referred back to as the process proceeds. Some clients decide to write out their anchor statement, others do not. There is no right or wrong way to prepare an anchor statement; nor are there any rules about their length. The exercise is, however, crucial in establishing what the client and their former spouse or partner are looking to achieve, which will act as a guide for them throughout the process itself.

9.2.2 Hotspots and rapport

It is also necessary to explore with the client at this point their fears and concerns, so as to be able to establish the client's 'hotspots', if there are any. Hotspots are referred to as the matters that are going to cause clients undue anxiety/upset if mentioned; perhaps even lead to them wanting to leave the process.

At this stage the collaborative lawyer is looking to build rapport with the client, and lay the foundation of working together with them in an open and constructive way, so they can engage effectively in the collaborative process. It is this relationship that is so vital as the process proceeds, as the collaborative lawyer and their client will be working closely as a team and also with their counterparts. The collaborative lawyer is also building up a picture of their client's concerns so these can be carefully explained to their counterpart when preparing for the first four-way meeting, enabling both lawyers to prepare for and deal with 'the tiger bursting out of the basement' later on.

The collaborative lawyer will also need to discuss with their client the basic principles of the collaborative process and the terms of the participation agreement, emphasising the importance of interest-based negotiation and acting in good faith. The client can be given a copy of the participation agreement to take away and consider in readiness for the first four-way meeting.

9.2.3 Legal advice

It appears that the misconception has arisen that the collaborative process is *advice-free* or certainly at the initial stages. As discussed more fully in **Chapter 5**, although one does not want the client to become entrenched in a certain position or mindset, which will impede and frustrate the collaborative process, clients will naturally be anxious about their legal rights and what they are entitled to. Collaborative lawyers should at this initial stage go through the legal advice in any matter and discuss the legal principles that apply to their client's circumstances. Clients should be aware of the court process timeline and the menu of orders that a court can make. The collaborative lawyer needs to provide the client with information so that they can then make an informed decision as to whether or not they actually want to pursue a case using the collaborative process. We are asking clients to make informed, self-determined decisions and they have to be aware of the alternatives, What is important is to give advice in a neutral and informative way and at the appropriate time.

It will also be useful to establish with one's client their general views concerning the future of the marriage and whether they are looking to achieve a separation or divorce, so they can be given general information about the processes involved. The client will need to be made aware that court proceedings are not issued during the collaborative process unless they are to initiate agreed proceedings for the purpose of obtaining a consent order. Clients must also be clear that neither collaborative lawyer is able to act for their client in contested proceedings and both lawyers have to withdraw from acting for their client if the process breaks down.

Throughout this initial stage the collaborative lawyer needs to review with the client whether the collaborative process is in fact the most suitable one for them, or whether another option may be more appropriate.

9.2.4 Pacing and agenda setting

Another key matter that needs to be addressed with the client, at this stage, is pacing. Some clients will be keen for matters to be resolved as quickly as possible; others may not. Divorce and separation are intensely emotional processes and all clients are likely to be wading through some part of the emotional quagmire they have to go through. One of the benefits of the collaborative law process is that it can proceed at a pace the clients choose. Given the current delays in obtaining court time, this can make the collaborative law process an attractive option. It is, however, important to explain to one's client that the process will proceed at a pace that meets everyone's needs. When acting for the successful businessman with a wife who has not been involved in dealing with the finances before, it is going to be necessary to explain to one's client that his wife is probably going to need to go through the financial information at a slower pace.

If the client has existing problems that need to be addressed as soon as possible, such as interim financial arrangements and/or day-to-day care of the children, these need to be identified. Urgent and pressing issues can then be put on the agenda for the first four-way meeting.

9.2.5 Team building

One also needs to discuss with one's client what professional support might be needed to assist the collaborative process. Where there are emotional and/or communication issues for example, the clients may wish to use a family consultant, or undertake some personal counselling. Tax advice may be required, financial advice and/or from an expert on options in respect of pensions. There may be issues over valuations in respect of businesses and/or properties. The principles of instructing other professionals jointly can be explained at this stage. Depending on the age of the children, the parties may wish to consider how the children's views should be canvassed and taken into account. The question of the team, which is an important aspect of the collaborative law model, is addressed in **Chapter 7**.

9.2.6 Explaining the next steps

Finally, one also needs to discuss with one's client what will happen next. This is likely to involve contacting the other collaborative lawyer who has been appointed or, if no collaborative lawyer has yet been instructed, writing an initial letter to their spouse or partner. Assuming another collaborative lawyer has been appointed you can confirm to your client that you will be making contact with them with a view to agreeing a date and venue for the first four-way meeting and an agenda. The agenda will also be agreed with the client. It is usual at the first four-way meeting for the agenda to cover such items as discussion of anchor statements; what professional support is needed; what homework and tasks the clients need to undertake before the next four-way meeting; going through, discussing and signing up to the participation agreement; the question of legal costs; and any urgent and pressing items which need immediate attention.

9.2.7 Preparing with your collaborative counterpart

If it is practically possible, before the first four-way meeting it will be beneficial if the collaborative practitioners can meet face to face to discuss the case. If you do not know the other collaborative lawyer, consider arranging to meet them beforehand so you can start to establish a relationship. If you cannot meet in person the lawyers will certainly need to discuss matters on the telephone, perhaps on several occasions. The collaborative practitioners can be said to offer the clients a mirror of working together collaboratively, so it is essential that they have a good working relationship. At this stage the collaborative practitioners need to:

1. Identify the clients' priorities.
2. Agree an agenda for the first four-way meeting (are there any urgent issues that need to be dealt with?).

3. Share the clients' anxieties and vulnerabilities.
4. Discuss the need for any interdisciplinary work or addition of other members of the team.
5. Consider the practicalities of meeting up – when and where, do not forget the food (biscuits, pastries, fruit, etc.).
6. Decide who is going to prepare the participation agreement.
7. Discuss whether any legal advice has been given to the clients and share this.

It is important that the most up-to-date version of the participation agreement is used. This can be accessed from the members' section of the Resolution website (**www.resolution.org.uk**). When an agenda has been agreed, it then needs to be confirmed and approved by each client.

The collaborative practitioners need to agree who will prepare the minutes in respect of the first four-way meeting and for subsequent meetings. It is common practice that collaborative practitioners share this role on an alternating basis. The collaborative practitioners should agree the minutes before they are sent out to either of the parties.

9.3 THE FIRST MEDIATION SESSION

The first tasks are to establish rapport with the parties and make sure the ground rules are understood and agreed. It is important to welcome each party, smile when greeting them and show them into the meeting room. It can assist in putting the parties at their ease to offer refreshments at this point and check with them if they wish to use first names all round. The mediator can also bring to the parties' attention the pads and pens provided for them to make their own notes to take away from each session if they wish.

At the start of the session it will be helpful for the mediator to give a brief overview of what is going to happen:

- discuss the agreement to mediate and ground rules;
- sign up to the agreement to mediate;
- explore and agree an agenda and priorities with the couple for that session;
- start to work through the agenda items.

9.3.1 The agreement to mediate

Having made sure each party has read the agreement to mediate and has a copy in front of them to consider, the mediator can then move on to outline the key points of the agreement, namely:

1. The mediator will help the parties arrive at their own informed decisions, not by arbitrating or making decisions for them, but by assisting them to explore their circumstances and their options.
2. The mediator acts in an impartial role. The mediator does not give legal advice but will provide legal information as necessary. The mediator will, however, comment if any proposed terms are likely to fall outside the parameters that a court might approve.
3. Mediation is a voluntary and non-binding process. The parties will need to take legal advice from their own solicitors on any consensus reached and should each take legal advice in any event as they wish during the process. If they reach a consensus their solicitors will advise them on how they are able to reach a binding agreement in due course, if this is what they wish to do. If their solicitors have questions, these can be dealt with in an additional mediation session if necessary.
4. Each party will be required to provide full financial disclosure for informed decision making. All financial disclosure is open whereas all discussions and attempts to resolve matters are privileged or without prejudice.
5. The mediator will treat the mediation as confidential, except in relation to any child or person being at risk of harm, which may be disclosed, but usually after first discussing this and also so far as the mediator has duties by law as laid down in the Proceeds of Crime Act 2002 and relevant regulations.

After any questions have been dealt with, the parties are then asked to sign the agreement to mediate. If the mediator has available three copies of the agreement to mediate, each party and the mediator can sign each copy. They then each have a signed copy for their records. Mediation cannot proceed if both of the parties are not willing to sign up to the agreement to mediate.

9.3.2 Setting the agenda/priorities

Once the agreement to mediate has been signed, the next step is for the mediator to agree an agenda with the parties and establish what their priorities are. If it has not already been done, the mediator also needs to confirm how long the parties wish to meet for. The recommended time for a session is usually one and a half hours, but by agreement shorter or longer sessions can be arranged.

From consideration of the preliminary information forms and from their initial contact, the mediator will have some understanding of the issues each party wishes to address and what they wish to achieve from the mediation process. The mediator has to exercise caution and care at this point, as there can be other underlying issues that surface as soon as the session progresses and one party may not be keen to address an issue that is crucial to the other party. The parties can also be very anxious and at different emotional stages at this point. There may be urgent issues and competing priorities. The mediator needs to discuss with the parties how to allocate the time, giving an even-handed approach to both parties and avoiding contention. Using a flip chart at this stage to write up agenda items can greatly assist. The mediator may need to ask a series of general and open questions to establish the current and background circumstances and explore with the couple what needs to be addressed. At this point the mediator needs to be wary of one or both of the parties trying to take control. It is the mediator's role to manage the process and prevent any hijacking of the session at this time.

There is no right or wrong order for dealing with matters. It may be sensible to start with discussions about whether the parties are looking at a separation, a divorce, or just wanting to discuss all their options. Whether there is to be a separation or divorce can influence the options available. The couple may however simply want general legal information at this point. It may then be prudent to move on to talk about the arrangements for the children and then to look at finances. It can assist the parties to work out the arrangements for the children first, before they move on to look at their financial position and how their resources are to be allocated. There is specific training available for those mediators who wish to include children in the mediation process.

Resolution mediators do not ask each party to make a presentation of their position at the beginning of the mediation, as is done in the commercial mediation field.

At this stage the mediator may choose to explore with the couple their overall objectives. These can then be written up on the flip chart, so they are always visible and can then be referred to at any point. A mediator will need to assess, from the level of conflict between the parties, whether raising the question of overall objectives at this point will assist.

9.3.3 Use of the flip chart

Using a flip chart may be new to mediators, but it is an invaluable tool. In a state of anxiety people do not always hear what is said and can easily forget. To have key points that the parties can look at throughout the session helps them focus. If you use different coloured pens for each party when charting up options for child care, it is easy for each party to see exactly how much time they might be spending with their child and hard to ignore the time the other party may be spending. Preparing a schedule of assets using the flip chart makes sure each party can see the level of their financial resources in front of them at all times. For some parties this may be the first occasion they have been aware of this information. If the flip chart is used the mediator needs to remember to display the relevant pages during each session.

9.3.4 Mediation Forms E

Where the parties have indicated they wish to look at financial issues, the first step will be for disclosure of their respective financial positions to take place. If the parties have not already completed their mediation Forms E, copies should be handed to them. The mediator can then explain what needs to be done and deal with any questions. An appointment for the next session with the parties can be scheduled in anticipation of when the Forms E will be available, or once they have been completed. If the parties have already exchanged Forms E between solicitors, copies can be arranged to be provided to the mediator and both of the parties, if this has not already been done. Copies of both Forms E need to be made available to each party. When going through the Forms E, information about the parties' capital, pensions and incomes can be put up on the flip chart, with a view to creating an open schedule of assets. If the parties decide they do not wish to complete Forms E (perhaps because of the simplicity of their financial position), or provide supporting documentary evidence, it is a matter for them, but the mediator should inform them that their respective solicitors will not be in a position to advise them if they are not satisfied that full and frank disclosure has taken place. Where the parties are very familiar with the family's finances they may not wish to go to the trouble of providing all the supporting documentary evidence normally required by Form E, such as 12 months' worth of bank statements, but wish it to be recorded that they will do so if this is required at a later date.

9.3.5 Ending the session

Before the end of the session the mediator needs to:

1. Agree an agenda with the parties for their next meeting.
2. Confirm what information and/or documents need to be obtained by each of the parties in readiness for the next session. In addition to completed Forms E, it may be necessary for one or both parties to check, for example: their entitlement to state benefits; their mortgage capacity; their ability to increase their earning capacity or obtain paid employment; their future monthly income needs; and the cost of meeting their housing needs.
3. Agree with the parties if they require a written summary of the meeting or not. This would normally be something they would pay for separately. At the end of the session in any event the mediator can prepare a copy of any information or figures from the flip chart and send it out to each party. Financial information is given on an open basis. However, discussions about arrangements for the children, housing options or suggested budgets should be marked 'without prejudice'.
4. Remind the parties of the option to seek independent legal advice between sessions. For those who are eligible for public funding remind them of the availability of the legal help with family mediation scheme.

5. Ask for payment of their fees for the session and/or a sum on account of costs.
6. Arrange a date and time for the next session.

9.4 THE FIRST COLLABORATIVE FOUR-WAY MEETING

9.4.1 Beginning the first meeting

It is likely that the clients will be somewhat anxious at the first four-way meeting and it is important to do as much as possible to put them at their ease. A warm welcome is essential. Some collaborative lawyers meet with each other before the first meeting, so when the clients arrive they can greet them together. At the start of the four-way both collaborative lawyers can speak about the benefits of the collaborative process. It may be useful to very briefly go over the meetings agenda so that the clients are again aware of what is going to happen. It is also important to invite the clients to express their objectives (anchor statements) in choosing the collaborative process. Practitioners should consider the benefits of writing a synopsis of the anchor statements up on the flip chart so that they can be seen by everyone throughout each meeting. The flip chart can then be put back up in the meeting room during further meetings so that, at any point in time, the clients can easily be reminded of what they want to achieve and what is important to them. If there are occasions when an impasse is reached (and there will be) the clients can be referred back to their anchor statements.

Although the collaborative process is there for the clients' benefit, it is the responsibility of the collaborative lawyers to maintain control of the meeting.

9.4.2 The participation agreement

After the clients have expressed their objectives in choosing the collaborative law process the participation agreement needs to be viewed and signed. Whether or not one reads through the entire agreement word for word is a matter of choice but key paragraphs should be referred to and discussed with the clients and full opportunity given to the clients to ask questions.

The key purpose of the first four-way meeting is to establish the ground rules, set the objectives and sign the participation agreement, whereby the parties confirm these understandings and bind themselves to them in front of each other.

9.4.3 Future tasks to undertake: bringing in other collaborative professionals; financial disclosure and homework

After the participation agreement has been signed, one can then move on through the agenda items. These are likely to include a general discussion about the future of the marriage and whether or not there should be a separation and/or divorce and also the options as to how this might be achieved. Consideration will need to be given as to how financial information should be provided. For most couples the exchange of completed Forms E is likely to be the most appropriate choice. The question of disclosure is considered in **Chapter 10**. If it is apparent at this stage that valuations will be needed in respect of properties and/or businesses or other items, how this is to be achieved can be discussed, together with the need for any involvement from other professionals. A list of homework tasks for the parties can be compiled and given to them at the end of the meeting.

Consideration also needs to be given to scheduling future four-way meetings. It is likely to be helpful if several future meetings can be organised well ahead for these to be booked into everyone's diaries. Before ending the meeting it is useful to review the progress that has been made.

Debriefing after the meeting with both your client and also your collaborative counterpart is vital. It is important to iron out any issues as soon as possible, particularly if you have not worked previously with your counterpart.

CHAPTER 10

Disclosure

William Hogg

It has to be impressed upon clients that neither mediation nor the collaborative process should be perceived as a soft option, and it should not be considered that it is safe in the process to deal with disclosure in anything but a full and rigorous way. These processes rely on giving the clients the right to self-determine whatever disclosure is required, but we have to ensure that clients are in a position where they have sufficient information to determine issues. It is therefore important that both of the clients and the lawyers acting for them should have a clear idea of the assets (or debts) involved. The role of disclosure in the collaborative process, and indeed in the mediation process, is to carry out a fact-finding orientation in a voluntary way that is vastly different from that used in the court process.

10.1 FORMS OF DISCLOSURE

In the court process we follow a process of disclosure that takes place in line with the court's norm. We have Form E, the Questionnaire, and inevitably a list of deficiencies. There may well be an application for a production appointment and, in international cases, an application for letters rogatory.

The procedure in both collaborative law and mediation is far more focused on the needs of the client and produces more clarity. It is normal in both processes to share either the collaborative Form E or the mediation Form E. The disclosure will usually be accompanied by the documentation that is supplied in the court process, although in the voluntary process it need not be restricted to a 12- month period. With their mediator in mediation and with their lawyers in the collaborative law process, the parties can agree disclosure in whatever way creates a safe and informed environment. Clients in mediation may also wish to refer this issue to their lawyer in between sessions. This produces a forum where information is shared and structured to suit the issues that have to be addressed. Generally we will be considering the following:

1. What information/more information do we need to achieve proper informed decisions?
2. What level of detail?
3. What documentary back up do we require?
4. What is the timescale for producing such documentation and information?
5. Who will draft the information summary/assets schedule?

10.2 POWER OF TEAMS

In the collaborative process particularly, the disclosure is often gathered by teams, i.e. the financial neutrals like accountants, independent financial advisers (IFAs), private bankers, valuers, etc., as discussed in **Chapter 7**. The power of the team assists both lawyers. The clients will appoint a single expert to advise on pensions, budgets, and even in some circumstances to prepare the initial Form E. This process frees up the expert to deal with disclosure in a very efficient and open way, producing information that is utilised by the team to work through the collaborative process. Mediation practices are different in that mediators will often provide information about the option of the parties instructing a joint expert and refer the parties back to their lawyers to seek advice on the provision of necessary information. Unlike the court process, this ensures that disclosure is not accidental and piecemeal but is produced in such a way that it can be brought to the meetings in a helpful, open way.

10.3 INFORMATION SHARING

In both the collaborative and mediation processes the financial information that is gathered is presented in a clear and precise way, usually utilising a flip chart to facilitate sharing information in a meeting.

In the collaborative process, it is often considered normal to have the experts who provided assistance present in the meetings so that a four-way meeting becomes a five-way or a six-way meeting depending on the number of team members involved. This not only provides clarity but ensures that during meetings information not regularly available can be obtained by the expert present at the meeting. In the collaborative process the information summary or asset schedule is prepared and again added to and utilised during the decision making process.

In respect of the mediation process, having a financial summary prepared is useful. It is utilised throughout and added to when further information comes in.

10.4 VERIFICATION

Mediators do not verify the completeness and accuracy of the information provided, but will try to help the clients identify what information and documents would help them resolve any issues and to consider how these may best be obtained.

The collaborative law disclosure process does rely on verification on the facts given. In the court process it is invariably difficult to get records going back beyond 12 months, but in both the collaborative and mediation process we find ourselves with a free hand obtaining information to confirm what is being said. We also must not lose sight of the fact that the clients may not require a level of disclosure that we as lawyers feel comfortable with. That is their choice as long as that choice is made with full knowledge of what information can be obtained and what information is available.

10.5 STATUS OF DISCLOSURE

In mediation the financial facts, including any schedule of assets, are set out in an open financial summary, which is not a without prejudice document, although the documents themselves remain without prejudice unless of course there is an agreement in writing effectively opening them up. Similarly, in the collaborative process the schedule of assets is open, although the documents themselves are normally without prejudice but are normally opened up when an agreement is made at the end of the process.

In both processes the budgets, unless marked without prejudice, are open but it seems to be becoming the norm that they are marked as such.

10.6 NON-DISCLOSURE

Non-disclosure in both the collaborative and the mediation processes can result in litigation, invalidating any agreement or any settlement entered into on the basis of the disclosure made. The likelihood of non-disclosure exists in each case that we deal with as lawyers. However, in the voluntary disclosure process we are invariably dealing with disclosure that is being looked at and examined forensically either by experts or alternatively by the client and their legal advisers in situ or when advising on a mediation summary, unlike the court process, which very much relies on asking the right questions. However, we must not be blind to the fact that non-disclosure does occur, and that disclosure needs to be explained and dealt with in a vigilant and appropriate manner.

CHAPTER 11

Closure

Joanne Edwards

11.1 WHAT IS MEANT BY CLOSURE?

The word 'closure' is capable of various interpretations. For some it simply means a bringing to an end and achieving a conclusion, in a way which is functional. For others, the meaning runs a little more deeply. It implies the achievement of a feeling of finality or resolution, especially after a traumatic experience. In the first sense, the word connotes creating a blockage; yet paradoxically in the second sense, it implies an unblocking.

The way in which clients (and their advisers) have conducted themselves during the process of collaboration or mediation will likely determine the interpretation which is placed on the word 'closure' in an individual case. It is to be hoped that the client who has avoided the court process will emerge from the experience feeling relatively unscathed and in need of closure only in the sense of drawing the process to an end.

However clients are feeling at the end of the process, it is important that in the euphoria of an agreement having been reached (or the disappointment of negotiations having broken down), the lawyers should not overlook the importance of the closure stage of the process. If an agreement has been reached, careful legal drafting and a consideration of the clients' emotional needs are needed in an effort to avoid problems further down the line. In the event of a breakdown in negotiations, in addition to addressing the clients' heightened emotional needs, thought needs to be given to interim issues and ensuring that the case is ready to be passed on to new solicitors.

In either instance, it is human nature to breathe a sigh of relief and move on to the next case before the clients are fully over the finishing line. However, to neglect to deal properly with the closure stage is to leave open all sorts of potential problems in the future.

11.2 CLOSURE IN THE LEGAL SENSE AFTER AGREEMENT HAS BEEN REACHED

The most obvious aspiration after an agreement has been reached, from both the clients' and the lawyers' perspectives, is to deal with the legal steps which need to be taken in order to achieve a binding financial (or other) order. The exact mechanics of how this will be achieved will, of course, depend upon the particular process through which the clients have passed. However, certain steps are common to all processes.

11.2.1 In the collaborative law process

Clients who have reached agreement during the course of the collaborative law process will have had the benefit of legal advice along the way, during the course of the four-way meetings. In a collaborative process which is working as it should, the two collaborative colleagues will have given most (if not all) of their legal advice within the four-way setting; and to the extent they have provided any advice to their individual clients outside the process, they will have compared notes, divulged the advice given and agreed a likely bracket of outcome. Similarly, advice from accountants, IFAs, valuers and the like will have been received in the four-way setting and any queries or doubts will have been addressed as they arose.

That being the case, it is likely in the collaborative process that the parties will have worked gradually towards an agreement, addressing along the way any potential question marks over enforceability, drafting points or the likelihood of the court approving any aspect of the agreement. As such, the closure stage in the collaborative process is likely to be shorter than in a case in which the parties have engaged in mediation.

In the penultimate four-way meeting, the parties will likely have spent time working towards heads of agreement and agreeing who is to draft more detailed minutes of agreement. That document will be produced prior to the final four-way meeting and will be circulated before that meeting for discussion and signature at the final meeting. That final four-way meeting will also address issues such as the drafting of a joint Form M1 for submission to the court; the application for decree absolute; agreement as to which firm is to lodge and oversee the progression of the proposed order, etc.

It is of particular importance that the minutes of agreement, once drawn, should include a recital indicating that the agreement has been reached through the collaborative law process. The judiciary has shown widespread approval of alternatives to court generally, and collaborative law specifically. The collaborative law process was expressly endorsed by Mr Justice Coleridge in *S* v. *P* [2008] 2 FLR 2040, in which the court approved a shortcut procedure for approving consent orders in the High Court following resolution of family issues through the collaborative law process. At county court level, there is diversity in approach across the country. In the Principal Registry there is no procedure for the fast-tracking of orders arrived at in the collaborative law process, although the district judges are fully conversant with and supportive of the process. Others have reported regional variations, with some local courts having a fast-tracking procedure in place.

However, it must be borne in mind that the mere fact of including in the minutes of agreement a recital to indicate that the agreement has been reached through the collaborative law process will not persuade the court to approve and make into an order an agreement which is fundamentally unfair to one of the parties.

11.2.2 Following mediation

Achieving closure in the legal sense following a successful outcome at mediation is, of course, markedly different in certain respects.

Most stark is the fact there is likely to be a long tail to implementation following a successful mediation. Although one would expect clients who have engaged in the mediation process to have taken legal advice outside the process, whether beforehand or during its currency, this is not universally the case. Some clients will only go and obtain legal advice once an understanding in principle has been reached in mediation and a memorandum of understanding drawn up by the mediator.

It is also fair to note that the clients' experience after the drawing up of a memorandum of understanding will largely depend upon the proactivity or otherwise of the mediator during the process, and the understanding which each client's solicitor has about mediation.

It is to be hoped that, during the mediation process, each client has been full and frank in the disclosure provided; and, in turn, the mediator has been reasonably robust in reality-testing the various options explored and has imparted an appropriate level of information as to whether a court would likely approve the detail of what is set out in the memorandum of understanding. In the unlikely event that these objectives have not been met, and an unworkable set of proposals is presented to the solicitors, the clients are likely to find themselves going back to the drawing board.

Another factor which can be determinative of clients' experience following mediation, and the time lag between the drawing up of a memorandum of understanding and the lodging of minutes of agreement at court, is the empathy which the solicitors asked to advise have in relation to mediation. Those who are fully supportive of alternatives to court will take great care to try to iron out any wrinkles in the proposals contained in the memorandum of understanding and generally to support and progress the stage at which the clients find themselves. Unfortunately, however, there are solicitors who will seek to unpick the work undertaken in mediation. To do so is undermining of the process and of the achievements of the clients.

Assuming that the legal advice provided post-mediation endorses the understanding in principle reached during the mediation process, time can be spent fleshing out during the drafting process any aspects of the proposed agreement which remain unclear. It may be that the memorandum of understanding sets out several different scenarios which the clients had been exploring in mediation, in which case the solicitors will help the clients work towards the most appropriate outcome for their family, with the benefit of legal advice. It may be that the clients decide to have a further session of mediation, armed with the advice they have received, to further whittle down the settlement options. Thereafter, the minutes and Forms M1 will be lodged at court and, ultimately, decree absolute applied for.

11.2.3 Practical considerations

Within the general heading of legal closure, there are some specific practical steps which can and should be undertaken at the closure stage in an effort to avoid problems arising in the future.

Detail of the drafting of the order

Lawyers drafting minutes of agreement at the conclusion of the collaborative process, or following the drawing up of a memorandum of understanding, should take great care at the drafting stage to avoid enforcement issues arising in the future. Although there are various cures, all involve the court. Clients who have reached agreement using an alternative dispute resolution (ADR) process are by definition unlikely to want to have to go down this route.

Therefore, the key to avoiding enforcement problems is prevention at the drafting stage. Orders should be prepared to ensure enforceability. They should be clear as to whom any obligation relates; what that person is to do; if a monetary payment, in what sum, by when and for how long; and otherwise, how is the obligation to be carried out and within what timeframe. Care must be taken to ensure that the court has power to order what has been agreed, and if not to record the relevant part of the agreement as recitals.

As the corollary to those aspirations, complexity in drafting is to be avoided, as is lack of clarity. Even following an ADR process, it is best to deal with as much as possible in the order, and not leave anything to be agreed between the parties in the future. To the extent that something is capable of being the subject of an order rather than an undertaking, it is the order route which should be taken. Finally, so as to reduce the scope for litigation against one party's estate in the future, it is better to avoid by way of security undertakings to leave by will and seek, for example, the taking out of a dedicated life policy.

Dealing with costs

Before concluding the drafting stage, it is sensible to deal with the question of costs head on.

Whether the clients have gone down the collaborative law route or attended mediation and then taken legal advice outside the mediation process, there may be an imbalance in the level of their costs. This may be because the parties have instructed firms with widely differing charge out rates; or it may be that, for emotional or other reasons, one party has been in contact with their solicitor much more than the other.

Rather than discovering, immediately before the implementation stage, that a joint account which was to be split equally between the parties has been hugely depleted by one party paying a legal bill which was unknown to the other, it is wise to address the issue of costs at the final four-way meeting or just before signing the minutes of agreement following the mediation process. Specifically, the lawyers involved should make clear to the clients not only the extent of any outstanding legal costs, but also the extent of time on the clock which has yet to be billed to the individual client, as well as an estimate of costs for implementing the order. There can then be a discussion as to whether the totality of the outstanding and projected costs on each side will simply come off the top of the pot for division; or whether, in the alternative, the sum of any difference between the level of legal costs incurred will come off the ultimate pot of the client responsible for that imbalance. In some collaborative law cases, the collaborative colleagues agree that they will each apply the same charge out rate in the particular case. However, this may not be possible in every area of the country, and still does not deal with the imbalance which arises as a result of varying levels of client contact. All of this reinforces the need for an open and timely discussion about the treatment of costs.

Interim arrangements

Even where agreement has been reached, there will likely be a number of weeks between the agreement being reached and it being drawn up into agreed minutes and, ultimately, approved by the court. In those circumstances, with the assistance of their lawyers the parties must agree whether any financial arrangements are to be implemented immediately, prior to confirmation that the order has been approved by the court and, if not, what the interim arrangements are to be. Similar considerations apply in respect of interim and longer-term arrangements for children.

11.3 CLOSURE IN THE LEGAL SENSE IN THE EVENT OF NEGOTIATIONS HAVING BROKEN DOWN

Arguably more complex is the question of achieving closure following the failure of the mediation or the collaborative law process.

Inevitably, clients will be experiencing a range of emotions at this stage. They will likely be disappointed that negotiations have broken down and will want to do some soul-searching as to the part they played in that failure. They will be disillusioned about the process and about the ability for a fair solution to be found. They will be feeling weary at what has passed already and will experience dread at the prospect of what lies ahead. Some will feel insecurity, either from a financial perspective of not knowing how their needs will be met on an interim basis, or from an emotional perspective of having to move on from a lawyer with whom they have formed professional bonds to a new lawyer. Understandably, many will feel anger and resentment, principally at their spouse.

The fact of these emotions being in play will likely make it more difficult for the mediator or collaborative lawyer to gauge how each client would like to move on and prepare for the next stage. As before, different considerations may apply depending upon the process used.

11.3.1 Following the breakdown of the collaborative law process

In the event of the collaborative law process breaking down in part or in full, it is a fundamental tenet of the standard participation agreement that the disqualification clause will kick in and each client will need to dis-instruct their solicitor and move on to a new solicitor if they wish to pursue litigation.

Before sending the file down to storage in those circumstances, the prudent collaborative lawyer would be wise to consider the following.

Passing on files to new solicitors

Following the breakdown of a collaborative law case, in the final four-way meeting the parties and the collaborative lawyers ought to have a discussion about the documents which are to be passed to any new solicitors in the case. In having that discussion, the collaborative lawyers will wish to balance a desire to provide sufficient information so that the clients avoid reinventing the proverbial wheel, with a desire to protect privileged information.

In those circumstances, it would be sensible to send to the new solicitors all of the financial disclosure provided during the collaborative process, together with any experts' reports obtained. It would also be helpful to provide the summary of financial discussions for the purposes of the financial dispute resolution (FDR) hearing, as referred to below.

Interim arrangements/partial agreements

Before passing on files, attention should be paid to any aspect of the case which can be salvaged for the clients. For example, it may be that they are able to agree and implement capital aspects, but that negotiations have broken down over maintenance. If that is the case, then it may be necessary to involve the court only to that narrower extent.

Even if there has been no element of overall agreement, it may be possible to agree a temporary solution as to the interim financial arrangements or interim arrangements for the care of the children. Again, if this is the case then this should be carefully recorded and conveyed to the new solicitors.

11.3.2 Following the breakdown of the collaborative process or mediation

Certain considerations following a breakdown in negotiations are common to collaborative law and mediation. They are outlined below.

Addressing issues of privilege

An area to which both mediators and collaborative lawyers have been giving much thought of late is the reach of privilege in respect of alternatives to court.

The question of a separate category of mediation privilege in family law cases has been the subject of some judicial scrutiny. A recent case in point is *Brown* v. *Rice* [2007] EWHC 625 (Ch), in which the court was invited to decide whether there is a distinct category of mediation privilege. In that case, mediation had been undertaken subject to the terms of a mediation agreement containing blanket confidentiality clauses and a clause to the effect that no binding agreement could arise until put in writing and signed. Although it was found that the confidentiality clauses bolstered the without prejudice privilege, ultimately it could not be treated as absolute. Specifically, it could not prevent the court from looking at documents produced during the mediation which had been created for other purposes; from hearing evidence as to whether an agreement had been reached; and it was found that the clause about the non-binding nature of any agreement unless put into writing and signed did not prevent the court from hearing evidence as to the question of whether it had been waived during the mediation.

In consequence of this, and other authorities, it is sensible for the agreement governing the ADR process to provide for a number of steps to be taken at the closure stage, including the creation of a summary document for any future FDR appointment; to stipulate that all negotiations are subject to contract, that agreements must be in writing and that there is to be no implied waiver of these stipulations; and, at the conclusion of each ADR meeting where no agreement has been reached, there ought to be a clear written acknowledgement, signed by both parties, to that effect.

In the same vein, although this will be covered by the participation agreement or the agreement to mediate, it would be prudent for clients to be reminded at the end of the process that anything said during the ADR process will remain subject to without prejudice privilege and that aspirational budgets or other documents created for the purpose of the ADR are covered by the privilege. It will only be financial and other documents with an existence separate from the ADR process which will generally be disclosable and, again, it would be wise to remind clients of this.

Clients should also be reminded that, in accordance with the standard participation agreement, the minutes of collaborative meetings are privileged. They are not only to be a record of events but to form part of the without prejudice communications between the parties.

Role of mediators/collaborative lawyers/other parties in any future litigation

It would also be prudent for advisers in a case where the negotiations have broken down to seek to reduce the risk of being compelled to give evidence in any litigation. This is best achieved by having a clause in the participation agreement or agreement to mediate in which the parties expressly record that they will not seek to call them, although ultimately the court will retain discretion. Again, it would be wise to reaffirm these principles at the end of the process.

Audit of one's own files

In any ADR process, there is a temptation to think that because there is no litigation involved, one does not need to take the same level of care over one's files. Specifically, in collaborative law proceedings the minutes of four-way meetings tend to be rather brief and to reflect not the (sometimes negative) aspects of the meeting during the course of which the clients were debating the pros and cons of a particular avenue, but rather the more positive aspects of the agreement actually reached. Similarly, in mediation any notes kept by the mediator tend to focus on arriving at a memorandum of understanding, and not on the difficulties encountered leading up to that point.

In either process, in the event of negotiations having broken down it is advisable for the individual collaborative lawyer or mediator to make a detailed, contemporaneous file note at the end of the process, summarising what were the issues which led to the process breaking down. In that way, if any uncertainty arises in the future (e.g. from a professional negligence perspective) it can be easily addressed from looking at the file.

Self-critique

Inevitably, where an ADR process breaks down the lawyers involved will wish to undertake a certain element of self-reflection.

In the collaborative process, the collaborative lawyers involved should arrange a final debrief during the course of which they reflect upon things they did well for their clients and things which, with the benefit of hindsight, they would have done differently. It sounds trite, but we have only been practising collaborative law in England and Wales since 2003 and we all have a great deal to learn.

Following a failed mediation, one ought to go back to one's mediation consultant and have a debrief with a more experienced practitioner as to particular aspects of the case which one has found difficult and how they may be better addressed in future cases.

11.4 EMOTIONAL CLOSURE

Whilst the importance of achieving closure from a legal perspective cannot be underestimated, nor should the importance of achieving emotional closure for clients.

Of course, one of the benefits for clients of choosing an ADR process is that they are able to dictate the pace at which the negotiations progress. One of the common reasons for clients experiencing difficulty in reaching agreement during the court process is that one party is anxious to proceed full steam ahead whilst the other has barely got over the shock of being served with a divorce petition out of the blue and is in no emotional state to engage at all, let alone in a rational and meaningful way.

In addition, there are various other long-term benefits to clients of a non-court-based approach:

- Mediation and collaborative law are client-centred processes and are not about taking sides and driving the parties further apart in a time of already heightened emotions.
- Good mediation and collaborative law should look to underlying problems of unresolved conflict and include a therapeutic element, if necessary with the input of a family consultant. It is not just about the legal outcome.
- Non-court-based processes can facilitate dialogue between parties where communication is dysfunctional due to the high emotions associated with family breakdown. Hopefully, this will be a lasting dialogue which will be of particular benefit where children are involved, as parents communicating can preserve parental roles.
- Mediation and collaborative law go beyond simply creating out-of-court settlements. They empower parties to take control of their own lives, as the process is driven by the parties themselves and not by a judge.

Because of these factors, it is to be hoped that clients will emerge from mediation or the collaborative law process in a better emotional state than would otherwise be the case. However, that is not universally the case. Some clients take longer to grieve than others and even allowing for the control they have over the pacing of the process and the therapeutic input received during its currency, they may still be feeling emotionally fragile by its end. For others, although the ADR process is empowering, it also brings out some very raw emotions. Others may have had to tackle a feeling of imbalance of bargaining power during the ADR process, which may have left them feeling rather drained.

To achieve emotional closure for our clients, therefore, we must ensure that we arm them with details of psychotherapists, counsellors, etc. to whom they can turn as the legal process comes to an end (if indeed they have not been seeking such help during the course of the process).

Coaching or counselling are especially useful in dealing with the various challenges presented by divorce and separation, notably:

- coming to terms with a new self-identity after divorce;
- dealing with the various choices associated with the financial aspects;
- children issues;
- grieving the death of the relationship;
- dealing with the impact of divorce on day-to-day life, e.g. having to come to terms with a new home, the children dividing their time between two parents, having to cut one's cloth financially, etc.;
- addressing low self-esteem issues arising from the divorce, especially where the client was a passenger rather than the driver.

Although counselling should be recommended in every case as a matter of course, it may be especially worth considering when the client is:

- having difficulty adjusting to change;
- making choices from anger rather than rational consideration;
- experiencing inability to make decisions;
- harbouring feelings of guilt;
- feeling issues around confidence;
- not showing signs of beginning to adjust to the new circumstances.

Emotional closure may also entail the collaborative lawyers or mediator losing all legal inhibitions at the last session and allowing the clients to say what they want to each other at the end of the process. This can be the most empowering aspect of either process for clients and may be the only way in which they will truly achieve closure.

It may be that other forms of support are appropriate. For example, clients may need support (individually or together) in understanding how their children are likely to react to their parents' separation and the life that lies ahead. In that case, it is wise to refer them on to Parenting after Parting classes. In the USA, separating couples sometimes achieve emotional closure by having a form of symbolic ceremony, such as planting a tree together. However, it remains to be seen whether such a form of closure will catch on in this country.

11.5 CONCLUSION

Arguably, from both legal and emotional perspectives, the closure stage of the ADR process is the most important from the clients' point of view. The skilled ADR practitioner will persuade the client to put to one side the elation associated with an agreement having been reached, or the negative emotions associated with breakdown in negotiations, and look to the future. In that way, with careful groundwork laid at this stage, the clients will be fully equipped to deal with whatever the future holds.

CHAPTER 12

Prenuptial and postnuptial agreements

Suzanne Kingston

Many practitioners will have noted the large increase in the number of prenuptial and postnuptial agreements they advise on and encounter within their practice. These agreements are now seen as an important feature in the wedding plans of many, not just celebrities who appear in *Hello!* The processes of mediation and collaborative law lend themselves well to dealing with these particular areas.

Of course practitioners are well aware of the fact that prenuptial and postnuptial agreements are not strictly legally enforceable in England and Wales. Until the Supreme Court judgment in *NG* v. *KR* can be considered fully, the extent to which the English courts are prepared to hold parties to the terms of such an agreement is unknown. The court is generally reluctant to have its jurisdiction ousted in divorce proceedings. It likes to retain jurisdiction to deal with potential awards without being fettered by agreements reached between the parties' prior to or after marriage. However, such an agreement may be considered by the court as evidence of the parties' intentions at the time that it was drafted and one of the circumstances of the case to take into account when considering financial settlements.

The government produced a Green Paper entitled *Supporting Families* (HO, 1998) in November 1998. Although the commentators believed that prenuptial agreements should become binding, this was not mirrored in the recommendations contained within the Green Paper. What the paper did was to set out circumstances in which a prenuptial agreement would not be legally binding including:

- if there were children;
- where one of the parties had not received independent legal advice;
- where the court considered that the enforcement of the agreement would cause significant injustice;
- where one or both of the parties failed to give full disclosure of assets and property before the agreement was made;
- where the agreement was made less than 21 days prior to the marriage.

Legislation has followed the Green Paper and indeed the Law Commission is undertaking a further review of prenuptial agreements which is due to report in 2012.

Although, at the moment, statute does not provide for legally enforceable agreements, there have been several important cases in this area which have developed and defined the way in which practitioners advise on and draft prenuptial agreements and have shaped how they are considered by the court.

12.1 THE CASE LAW

12.1.1 *K* v. *K*

Perhaps the most significant of the cases is *K* v. *K (Ancillary Relief: Prenuptial Agreement)* [2003] 1 FLR 120. This case concerns a short marriage lasting only 14 months in which elements of the prenuptial agreement were upheld by the court. Of most significance for practitioners was the checklist of factors that came out of this case and which the court felt should be considered where parties had entered into a prenuptial agreement and the court was being asked to consider the weight that should be given to that agreement:

1. Did the wife/husband understand the agreement?
2. Was she/he properly advised as to its terms?
3. Did she/he put him/her under any pressure to sign it?
4. Was there full disclosure?
5. Was she/he under any other pressure?
6. Did she/he willingly sign the agreement?
7. Did she/he exploit a dominant position either financially or otherwise?
8. Was the agreement entered into in the knowledge that there would be a child?
9. Have any unforeseen circumstances arisen since the agreement was made that would make it unjust to hold the parties to it?
10. What does the agreement mean?
11. Does the agreement preclude an order for periodical payments for her/him?
12. Are there any grounds for concluding that an injustice would be done by holding the party to the terms of the agreement?
13. Is the agreement one of the circumstances of the case to be considered under s.25 of the Matrimonial Causes Act (MCA) 1973?
14. Does the entry into this agreement constitute conduct which it would be inequitable to disregard under s.25(2)(g) MCA 1973?

There have been three important cases in 2007 and 2008 that have further developed this area of the law.

12.1.2 *Crossley* v. *Crossley*

In the case *Crossley* v. *Crossley* [2007] EWCA Civ 1491, [2008] 1 FLR 1467 the parties had considerable independent wealth at the time they met in June 2005. Mr Crossley had a fortune of around £45 million and Mrs Crossley had assets of around £18 million. The couple entered into a prenuptial agreement and married seven weeks later on 6 January 2006. The agreement provided that each would walk away from the marriage with whatever they had brought into it.

The marriage broke down after a year with the wife applying for ancillary relief claiming that her husband had not fully disclosed his assets when the agreement was entered into. The husband responded by issuing a summons requiring his wife to show cause why her ancillary relief claims could not be resolved in accordance with the terms of the agreement.

The husband argued at the first directions appointment (FDA) that, taking into account all the circumstances of the case, including the short length of marriage, the fact that they did not have children together and were independently wealthy, the wife should be held to the agreement.

The court directed that due to the exceptional facts of the case it was justified in limiting the financial disclosure. The parties were not required to attach supporting documentation to their Forms E and the wife was only entitled to raise an informal questionnaire. The matter was listed for a one-day final hearing.

The wife appealed to the Court of Appeal claiming that she had been denied the right to effectively present her case. Although this relates only to a procedural matter, and the wife later withdrew her application, the grounds on which her appeal was unanimously rejected are noteworthy. It was said that:

- Whilst the existence of the agreement cannot oust the court's obligation to apply the s.25 MCA 1973 factors, the exceptional facts of this case give rise to a 'very strong case that a possible result of the section 25 exercise would be that the wife receives no further financial reward'. 'If ever there is to a paradigm case in which the court will look to the prenuptial agreement as a factor of magnetic importance, it seems this is just such a case'.
- The court's overriding objective to deal with cases justly trumped the requirements to file Forms E with attachments and to permit formal questionnaires.
- Thorpe LJ remarked on the growing importance, in his view, of prenuptial agreements: 'It does seem to me that the role of contractual dealing, the opportunity for the autonomy of the parties, is becoming increasingly important'.
- In these exceptional circumstances the wife would in effect be required to show cause why the agreement should not rule the outcome of the ancillary relief claim.

In giving the rulings Thorpe LJ said that there was 'a strong argument' for legislation to clarify the position of prenuptial agreements.

However, this shift towards enforcing the terms of prenuptial agreements may be short lived as a result of the cases of *MacLeod* v. *MacLeod* [2008] UKPC 64 and *NG* v. *KR (Prenuptial Contract)* [2008] EWHC 1532 (Fam).

12.1.3 *MacLeod* v. *MacLeod*

In the case of *MacLeod* v. *MacLeod* [2008] UKPC 64 the couple signed a prenuptial agreement on the day of their marriage. During the course of their marriage they then signed two postnuptial agreements. The husband was significantly wealthier and older than the wife and they had five children during their nine-year marriage.

The final postnuptial agreement, which was the agreement that concerned the courts, provided for:

- each party to retain their separate property, which they had bought into the marriage;
- post-acquired property to be dictated by legal title;
- each party to waive their rights to maintenance;
- the children's expenses to be the responsibility of the parent with whom they lived although the husband would pay their educational expenses;
- the husband to pay the wife a lump sum calculated as $25,000 for each full year of marriage;
- the husband to pay the wife a lump sum of £250,000 for her to invest;
- the husband to pay all the expenses of the wife obtaining another degree (up to £100,000);
- the husband's half share in a property known as Dove's Hill to be conveyed to the wife (the intention being that this would be the home of her and the children);
- the husband to pay a monthly allowance of $3,000 for the benefit of the wife's grandmother;
- the wife to receive £1,000,000 in the event of divorce.

On the breakdown of the marriage the husband's assets totalled £13,810,000 and the wife's £184,000.

The wife argued that any prior agreements should be disregarded and she should be provided with full financial provision. The husband claimed that the final agreement should be upheld, although he accepted that there should be periodical payments for the benefit of the children while they lived with the mother. He also accepted that Dove's Hill was not a suitable home for the children and proposed an additional £750,000 to be used to buy another house, which would be held on trust until the youngest child had finished full-time education.

Although the judge at first instance said that he was 'satisfied that the wife agreed to the 2002 variation [second postnuptial agreement] freely, voluntarily and with full understanding thereof and having had proper legal advice, which she chose not to follow', he varied the agreement, providing the wife with an additional £1,250,000 lump sum. He rejected the idea of a trust and ordered periodical payments for the children, at the level proposed by the husband (£300 per child per calendar month).

Both parties appealed this decision. The wife repeated her claim for £5,000,000 for herself and £600 per month per child. Although the husband accepted the housing fund should be £1,250,000 he maintained that this should be held in trust.

The appeal and cross-appeal were both dismissed. However, the husband appealed further to the Privy Council on the issue of whether the £1,250,000 should be paid as a lump sum or on a trust basis. The Privy Council substituted a trust arrangement for the lump sum.

In its judgment the Board stated that, 'it is not open to them to reverse the longstanding rule that ante-nuptial agreements are contrary to public policy and thus not valid or binding in the contractual sense'. The Board pointed out what it saw as an 'enormous difference' between prenuptial and postnuptial agreements.

An explanation for this distinction is found in statute. A postnuptial agreement is a financial agreement made between spouses and therefore a maintenance agreement under s.34 MCA 1973 and prima facie binding although capable of being varied under s.35 MCA 1973.

It appears, on this basis, that postnuptial agreements could be said to be binding subject to the normal laws of contract and the court's power under s.35 to vary the agreement if it is found that there was a change in circumstances that justified an amendment or that the agreement did not contain proper financial arrangements with respect to any child of the family. In terms of what constitutes circumstances that justify a variation, the Board endorsed comments made in the case of *Edgar* v. *Edgar* [1980] 1 WLR 1410 recognising that family relationships are not like straightforward commercial relationships. It was said that, 'we must assume that each party to a properly negotiated agreement is a grown up able to look after him- or herself. At the same time we must be alive to the risk of unfair exploitation of superior strength'. It was said in *MacLeod* that, 'the mere fact that the agreement is not what a court would have done cannot be enough to have it set aside'. In this case, however, the agreement did not even purport to contain proper provision for the children and clearly the court had to provide for them.

In light of this case, it would seem advisable to consider making an agreement, prior to marriage, to sign a postnuptial agreement rather than relying on a prenuptial agreement being upheld. However, this case was focused primarily on the terms of a postnuptial agreement and the following case of *NG* v. *KR* perhaps puts the breaks on this apparent regression in the area of prenuptial agreements.

12.1.4 *NG* v. *KR*

The facts of *NG* v. *KR (Prenuptial Contract)* [2008] EWCA Civ 1304 are as follows:

- The husband was a French national and the wife a German national.
- They were married in London in 1998, where they continued to reside after their marriage, apart from a brief period in the USA.
- Their marriage broke down in 2006.
- The husband was still living in London at the time of the divorce proceedings, the wife moved to Germany in 2008.
- They had two daughters, aged six and nine years old, who were both born in London and who had lived in London with their parents until 2008 when they moved with their mother to live in Germany.
- At the time of the divorce the husband had little or no capital assets and, having previously worked during the marriage as a banker, was in the process of completing a PhD in biochemistry.
- The wife had substantial, immediately liquid assets of £54 million and shareholdings in two family businesses of substantial but undetermined value, all of which had emanated from her family.
- Four months before their marriage the parties entered into a prenuptial agreement drawn up under German law by a notary which did not fulfil the requirements of *K* v. *K* and which prevented either party from making a claim against the other for financial relief in the event of a breakdown of their marriage.
- The judge awarded a lump sum of £5,560,000 to the husband and periodical payments to him for each of the girls and provision by the wife of accommodation in Germany available to the husband for the purposes of visiting them in Germany.

Although the judge took the view that the husband should not be held to the terms of the agreement, she did, nonetheless, take the view that the content of the document should be persuasive and she assessed the husband's award at the bottom of the bracket of his claims on the basis of needs as a result of his entering into the agreement. It was considered relevant that the assets in this case had emanated from the wife's family in the form of cash and investments and her shareholdings in the two family businesses.

Although the prenuptial agreement had been validly executed under either French or German law it did not fulfil the requirements of *K* v. *K* for the following reasons:

- The husband had not been provided with an opportunity to obtain independent legal advice upon its contents.
- The wife had not provided financial disclosure of her assets.
- There had been no opportunity to enter into negotiations between the parties as to the content of the agreement.

- The agreement did not envisage the arrival of their two daughters.
- The terms of the agreement were manifestly unfair.

Notwithstanding the above, the judge took the view that, even if the husband did not understand in detail the content of the agreement, he knew that he was giving up claims as a result of his entering into the agreement and that the terms of the agreement should, in effect, act as a sheet anchor on the full extent of his claims.

The wife appealed against the judgment on the basis that the court should have placed much greater weight upon the agreement and in fact should have held the husband to its terms.

On 2 July 2009 the Court of Appeal handed down its judgment and it remains the leading authority on how the courts should view the existence of a prenuptial agreement when deciding how parties' assets should be divided on divorce.

In commenting on the position of prenuptial agreements in England generally, the Court of Appeal was of the view that the law should uphold agreements made freely between adults and that England was out of sync with most of Europe in this regard. They went on to say that 'decisive weight' must now be given to the terms of a prenuptial agreement. The court had clearly formed a strong view on this matter as it went so far as to call for legislation to introduce a formal presumption that both pre- and postnuptial settlements be 'dispositive' of any claim. This means that the agreement should form the basis of any award made by the court.

One of the central issues that the Court of Appeal had to consider was whether the husband should be held to the terms of the agreement, even though he had not received full disclosure of the wife's assets and had not received independent legal advice. Following the guidelines given in *K* v. *K* practitioners generally considered such conditions to be basic requirements for an agreement to be included as one of the factors to be taken into account by the court upon divorce. However, the court found that the husband, an international banker at the time, had had plenty of opportunity to obtain legal advice, even if he had then chosen not to do so. Furthermore, they found that he was aware that his wife was significantly wealthy even though he had not received full financial disclosure and had chosen not to negotiate the terms of the agreement.

As a result the husband's claim was significantly reduced with the Court of Appeal awarding the husband a housing fund of £2.5 million on the basis that this is held on trust for the children during his parenting years. Similarly, his capitalised income fund was reduced to cover his needs only until the youngest child reached 22 years of age.

As the court was considering an agreement drawn up in Europe, it commented that due weight needs to be given to the marital property regime that the parties selected in their agreement. Some commentators have questioned whether the agreement in this case would have been upheld to the extent that it was had it been drawn up in England, where marital property regimes do not exist, unlike in most of Europe.

In March 2010 the Supreme Court considered the husband's appeal of this decision and the judgment is being eagerly awaited by practitioners. Until this judgment can be considered fully, the extent is unknown to which the English courts are prepared to hold parties to the terms of an prenuptial agreement even where the *K* v. *K* requirements are not adhered to as in this case.

It is thought unlikely that the Supreme Court will take the opportunity to address the anomaly that currently exists in English law where prenuptial agreements are not legally binding whereas postnuptial agreements (as in *Macleod*) potentially are. As the enforceability of prenuptial agreements is a matter for Parliament, and not the courts, they are more likely to comment on the need for the government to legislate in this area following the Law Commission's report into this area, which is due in 2012. Some commentators are of the view that the Court of Appeal might uphold the lower court's decision on the basis that it can distinguish this case because it involves foreign parties who entered into a German agreement but that they will reiterate the need for the basic requirements set down in *K* v. *K* to be met if parties wish for their agreements to be given 'decisive weight' by the courts. Whether that is indeed their view is yet unknown, and until the judgment has been handed down, practitioners must still exercise great caution when advising in this area.

Indeed, many solicitors take the view that they ought to consider noting prenuptial agreements as high risk matters on their firm's central registers and making sure that their insurers are aware of any prenuptial or postnuptial agreements that they are advising on. The aim of this is of course to ensure that the firm has adequate cover in place for these high risk cases. Taking steps to limit liability at the outset of the case, in a client care or disclaimer letter for example, is also a precaution that may be worth considering.

What is clear is that this remains one area of the law which needs to be treated with utmost caution.

12.2 WHEN IT WOULD BE SENSIBLE TO CONSIDER HANDLING A PRENUPTIAL AGREEMENT COLLABORATIVELY

It is important when considering whether prenuptial or postnuptial agreements should be drafted collaboratively that clients are properly screened. Broadly, the sorts of clients who would suit the collaborative law process are people who would like to, and are able to, generate their own options and who would wish to play a greater role in finding their own solutions. The process gives clients the opportunity to be creative and flexible in terms of the outcome and solutions that are reached.

When initially discussing matters with a client it is sensible to consider whether that client is able and intends to participate in the process in good faith, and whether both parties are suitably committed to the collaborative process. The sorts of things the lawyer should consider when screening clients are:

- Has the client got an ability to participate in good faith?
- Has the client an ability to see perspectives beyond their own?
- Has the client a belief in the future?
- Does the client accept the negatives while also being able to search for the positives?
- Can the client acknowledge the views and needs of others?

It is imperative that the solicitors involved in a collaborative law case are able to spend time at the beginning of the process listening carefully to the clients, understanding their hopes and fears and explaining very carefully to the clients how the process works.

12.3 WHERE THE COLLABORATIVE PROCESS IS NOT RIGHT

The collaborative process is not right for every case or every client. It is important that solicitors accept this and only encourage clients to sign up to the collaborative law process where it is appropriate for the case in question.

The process will not be right for cases where:

- there is a high level of conflict and distrust between the parties;
- clients do not want to provide information or disclosure;
- there may be third party pressure, e.g. from a new partner or relative.

12.4 SO HOW DOES THE PROCESS WORK?

12.4.1 The client interview

During the first interview a solicitor goes through the various process options with the client, including the collaborative law process, and ascertains whether or not that process is suitable. The screening process set out above will help establish whether or not the collaborative law process is appropriate.

Presupposing it is agreed by the solicitor and client that the case is suitable for the collaborative law process, then the solicitor will take detailed instructions from the client about what they would like to achieve in the collaborative law process and will probably work on points to include in an agenda to be discussed with the solicitor representing the other party.

In terms of preparing a prenuptial agreement the aim would be for the clients either:

(a) to reach an agreement directly between themselves without the help of a lawyer and for the lawyers to then help refine and finalise the agreement and put it into effect by drafting a prenuptial agreement; or
(b) to negotiate the terms of the agreement from scratch within the collaborative process and then go on to draft the agreement within the process.

Solicitors will then arrange a solicitor-to-solicitor meeting or telephone call to set out the parameters of the first meeting.

12.4.2 Lawyer-to-lawyer meeting/telephone call

The solicitors either meet together in one office or alternatively have a conference call to determine the agenda for the first meeting. Typically an agenda would be agreed and circulated as a four-way email to both solicitors and both clients prior to the first meeting.

The agenda is likely to include the following:

- discussion about the collaborative process and answering questions the parties have about the process;
- going through the participation agreement which is a specific agreement that would be modified to deal with prenuptial agreements: the parties need to sign up to this agreement at the outset of the process (see below);
- sharing of the parties' mission or anchor statements (see below);
- giving joint legal advice about how the courts treat prenuptial agreements in England and Wales;
- consideration of the hopes and expectations of the clients in drafting a prenuptial agreement;
- consideration of what will be required in terms of drafting, including a consideration of the financial information that would be required from the parties.

Once the solicitors have agreed an agenda, they will circulate it together with a joint preliminary letter, from both solicitors to both clients.

Typically, all communication in the collaborative process is undertaken by four-way emails to ensure that there is full transparency between the solicitors and clients and little room for misunderstanding since all of the information has been circulated to everybody. Of course there may be occasions where there will be separate privileged solicitor–client correspondence and discussion but in the main solicitors dealing in the collaborative forum have found that it is beneficial to have open lines of communication wherever possible so that trust in the process and in each other is built as an early foundation.

The initial letter of orientation to be sent to both clients is set out in Annex A to the Resolution prenuptial participation agreement. This can be modified for circulation to the clients in each case to take into account the particular circumstances of their case.

Resolution has now drafted prenuptial participation agreements which provide for couples with or without children, which will be the documents that the parties and the lawyers sign when engaging in the collaborative process. Copies of these documents appear on the members' section of the Resolution website (**www.resolution.org.uk**). It is imperative that the clients fully understand this document and a considerable amount of time should therefore be spent at the outset of the first meeting going through its contents. It is particularly important that the parties appreciate the consequences, in terms of the options available to them and the cost implications, of the collaborative process breaking down. In the case of prenuptial agreements it is likely that if negotiations break down then either an agreement will not be signed and/or the marriage will not take place (in most other collaborative situations, where the process breaks down, the case would then be likely to proceed to litigation and may end up in court).

Anecdotally, the lawyers who are involved in the collaborative law process have found that it is more successful if the clients draft either separately or together an anchor or mission statement, which sets out specifically what their goals and aspirations are for dealing with matters collaboratively.

These anchor statements can then be referred to later on in the process if there are any issues that become difficult to negotiate. Typically, the sorts of things that a client will say is that they want to pursue matters collaboratively since they want to ensure that they deal with their prenuptial agreement in the most dignified way possible and with a view to moving into a marriage that is transparent and open. Ground rules for how the marriage will work are set out in the negotiation process surrounding the drafting of the prenuptial agreement.

12.4.3 The first four-way meeting

In the first four-way meeting the clients and the lawyers tend to work through the agenda that has been set. There is a discussion about the collaborative process and what it means and it is for the lawyers to ensure that clients understand that this is an integrative interest-based negotiation and that solicitors and the parties will be working together in a constructive and respectful way.

The lawyers will go through the participation agreement highlighting the main clauses, and will set out how they intend to deal with the meetings and what is meant by negotiation in good faith.

It is important that the lawyers explain that, although financial information is open information, and is disclosable into court proceedings if the collaborative process breaks down, any details of the negotiations will be without prejudice and will not be disclosable.

The lawyers will explain that the collaborative process is a voluntary process and that if either party wishes to withdraw from it there is normally a 21-day cooling off period, although that timeframe can be reduced by agreement.

Once the lawyers are clear that both parties fully understand the terms and parameters of the discussions and negotiations, everybody signs the participation agreement, which then becomes the contract between the lawyers and parties in the process and signifies how matters will be conducted going forward.

An opportunity is then given to the clients to set out their anchor or mission statements and to explain their hopes and aspirations for both their relationship and this process. Although some clients feel it is not necessary to have these statements recorded, experience has shown that it can become invaluable in situations where there are real difficulties between the parties later on in the process.

This meeting often gets to a point where the lawyers can provide joint legal advice as to how prenuptial agreements are viewed in England and Wales, and describe the different types of agreement that may be considered, e.g. simple ring-fencing of pre-acquired assets or alternatively a more complex future-focused agreement where provision is made for the weaker economic party perhaps on a sliding scale with reference to the length of the marriage and any children that are born.

This often leads to general discussion about the type of agreement that the clients would like to have prepared and the key elements or provision that they wish to incorporate in that agreement in addition to how financial disclosure is to be dealt with.

Finally, the lawyers and parties will work together to establish what needs to be attained and in what timeframe, and any 'to do' list that is drafted becomes the homework for the next meeting and generally forms the agenda for that meeting.

12.4.4 Debrief meeting with clients

Following the first four-way meeting, each lawyer then tends to have a debriefing meeting with their client to ascertain how they found the first four-way meeting and to consider any issues or problems that they have with the process at this stage.

This is a sensible opportunity to discuss whether or not the prenuptial agreement is likely to be drafted in the collaborative law process by committee, or whether the lawyers will be drafting it and presenting it to the parties for their consideration. The former is inevitably a more time-consuming and therefore costly method of dealing with the drafting.

12.4.5 Further lawyer-to-lawyer meetings

A further lawyer-to-lawyer discussion follows, to work out how the lawyers are going to best address all of the client's needs within the process. This will often include the preparation of an agenda for the next session and considering any drafting points that may need to be undertaken in intermediate four-way meetings.

In between four-way meetings the agreed agenda is circulated by way of a four-way email together with the notes of any previous meetings (once approved by both lawyers). It is beneficial to have a fifth person in each meeting to take a note as this enables the lawyers to concentrate on the discussion and will ensure that a detailed note is taken of what is said and can be referred back to at any point in the future (for this reason it should, as mentioned above, be approved by both lawyers and perhaps clients).

At the start of each meeting, the lawyers confirm the agenda with the clients and check whether there are any new issues which have arisen and need to be addressed.

At this point, parties should be discussing the terms of the prenuptial agreement and financial disclosure.

12.4.6 Impasse strategies

Obviously, not every meeting is plain sailing. At times solicitors need to consider various strategies to move parties beyond an apparent impasse, including the following:

- Brainstorming to develop options and think creatively about solutions.
- Considering what matters most to each individual client and then looking at how best to effect compromise for the clients.
- It may be that the lawyers do not necessarily agree about how the prenuptial agreement should be drafted. If this is the case they will need to explain their respective positions to the clients in a four-way meeting. This maintains the transparency of the process and makes it clear to the clients that there may be a slight difference of opinions when drafting these documents. Clients should be provided with the potential outcomes and compromises which could be reached in order to finalise the terms of the document. Lawyers should explain that the court may have differing opinions as to prenuptial agreements and how they should be structured. This helps the clients understand the range of possibilities that may result if the court were asked to consider the terms of a prenuptial agreement in proceedings in due course.

12.4.7 The final four-way meeting

Prior to the final four-way meeting the lawyers will ensure that all documents, including the final version of the prenuptial agreement and schedules of disclosure, are ready for signing and approval by the clients.

At the meeting the lawyers and clients will review and sign the documents together and discuss any possible future pitfalls.

The lawyers will ask how the clients would like to deal with matters going forward and in particular to consider whether they would like to revisit any issues in the collaborative process if there are matters that need further discussion or consideration at some stage in their marriage, e.g. if the clients have agreed to review the agreement at any point in the future.

Finally, the lawyers will draw the collaborative process to a respectful and appropriate conclusion making sure at all times that they remember that this is a major life event for their clients and that they feel content with how the process has been used to reach settlement terms in relation to their prenuptial agreement.

12.5 FURTHER POINTS TO NOTE

Normally speaking discussions pertaining to prenuptial agreements will be marked 'without prejudice' and treated as such. However, when the prenuptial agreement has been signed then it is commonplace to open up the negotiations, which would include the minutes taken at the four-way meetings.

As well as prenuptial and postnuptial agreements, it is possible for the collaborative law process to be used for preregistration agreements in civil partnerships or cohabitation agreements. Indeed, many clients say they feel it is preferable to use the collaborative process for drafting these sorts of documents (which are often drafted at the beginning of their relationship) as it is seen as a much less antagonistic forum.

There are a number of barristers who are trained in collaborative law who may be able to assist with the drafting of these documents.

As well as English prenuptial agreements it is of course possible to deal with international prenuptial agreements on a collaborative law basis. Indeed, in most countries there are fully trained collaborative lawyers willing and able to help. It is imperative that lawyers consider at the outset of each case whether or not there are relevant jurisdictions outside England and Wales that should be considered. It may be that foreign advice is necessary and a mirror agreement in another jurisdiction may be required.

12.6 TOP TIPS FOR COLLABORATIVE PRENUPTIAL AND POSTNUPTIAL AGREEMENTS

Finally, some top tips, or key points to bear in mind, when advising on and drafting prenuptial or postnuptial agreements within the collaborative process.

- Screen potential clients carefully before encouraging them to engage in the collaborative process.
- Inform your insurers when you take on a new prenuptial or postnuptial case.

- Consider whether it is necessary to limit your liability, by way of a client care letter and/or disclaimer letter signed by the client.
- Decide whether or not it is necessary to obtain counsel's advice (this may provide added protection in terms of your firm's exposure) and consider if this advice should be obtained jointly or independently (and then disclosed within the collaborative process).
- Consider whether there are any other jurisdictions which may be relevant. If necessary obtain foreign advice and/or instruct foreign lawyers to advise on the position in that jurisdiction and/or to draft a mirror agreement. Consider whether this advice can be obtained jointly or if it should be a single instruction (and then disclosed within the collaborative process).
- Comply with the criteria set out in *K* v. *K;* however, in view of *MacLeod* v. *MacLeod* also consider whether or not a postnuptial agreement would in fact be appropriate and provide additional protection in the particular case.
- Ensure that a comprehensive note is taken at each meeting and is subsequently approved by all parties present at that meeting. This can then be referred back to at a later date if there is any disagreement about discussion that took place.
- Spend time at the final four-way meeting going through each term of the agreement and ensure there is a clear note of this to avoid a situation where a client could say at a later date that they had not understood any of the terms or the implications of those terms.
- Record the parties' anchor or mission statements at the outset so that these can be referred back to if necessary during the process.
- Bear in mind that although without prejudice during the collaborative process, the discussions and notes of meetings are likely to be opened up once the agreement has been signed.
- Ensure that there is sufficient time for the process to be properly conducted and for the parties to consider the terms that are being discussed prior to the wedding date (in the case of a prenuptial agreement) and be alive to the added pressure that one party may feel to sign up to the agreement.

CHAPTER 13

International disputes

Tom Amlot and Suzanne Kingston

The benefits of choosing either of the principal alternative dispute resolution (ADR) processes – mediation or collaborative law – in the context of an international dispute are obvious, but it is worth exploring them a little in the first part of this chapter. We will go on to address some of the difficulties posed to the international practitioner, particularly in the context of collaborative law, but none of these should deter professionals whose preference is to adopt an ADR process from doing so where it feels right for the client.

Some of the benefits – such as improved communication between the parties; the fact that the dispute shifts from being conducted on a rights to interest-based approach; greater certainty of outcome; and saving the client time and money – are dealt with in the following chapters.

13.1 COMMUNICATION

Communication, it might be said, is the biggest challenge facing a separating couple and ADR processes of course are aimed at encouraging and supporting communication rather than allowing clients to avoid communicating directly by ceding ownership of their issues to their lawyers. Communication is even harder in the context of a dispute with an international dimension because not only is there likely to be a geographical barrier reducing the opportunity for face-to-face communication between clients, but frequently we find there are cultural issues in play as well. So often, and so regrettably, children will lose frequent quality contact with one parent if they are abroad, and the tone may well be set for the co-parenting relationship during the legal mechanics of separation.

But a commitment to use direct communication through mediation or collaborative law is an excellent start on the road to better co-parenting in cases with an international dimension. It is suggested that there is no excuse in the second decade of the twenty-first century for failing to use technology to the maximum, so, e.g. a three-way meeting with a mediator by video conference should not now be something that should be regarded as inconvenient, expensive or difficult to organise.

Similarly, in collaborative law, four-way meetings via video link should not hold any fear for a competent and confident collaborative practitioner.

It is suggested that, if at all feasible, face-to-face meetings are preferable but if this does cause logistical and cost issues then video linking, followed by telephone conference calls are the next best thing. With the collaborative process there is scope for interweaving video conference/conference calls and face-to-face meetings which can produce a very effective process.

13.2 INTEREST-BASED APPROACH

With an international dispute, the scope for clients descending into rights-based negotiation is heightened from the start. It is drilled into family lawyers from an early stage that when a client comes into your office and there is an international dimension, a red flashing alarm bell should be metaphorically ringing loud and clear. It can be easy for the lawyer to slip into very directive and positional advice, and for the client to follow their lead in a rush to file divorce proceedings in order to seize jurisdiction. Most family lawyers have in their mind that this is a legitimate exception to Resolution and Law Society guidelines to issue all proceedings on notice, and therefore consider that they are doing the right thing in acting quickly and decisively. Yet arguably this approach of *issue first, talk later* goes against the very essence of ADR processes in general and collaborative law in particular.

The reality, of course, is that an international family is just as likely to benefit from an ADR process as any other family, and arguably more so if they have the sizeable resources which reflect the decision to relocate overseas for greater remuneration. And if they have had the resourcefulness to adapt to a different country in the past, it may well be that this trait is an invaluable resource in the dispute to be tapped into and harnessed in order to break sideways out of impasses and give the couple autonomy and ownership of their own solutions.

13.3 CERTAINTY OF OUTCOME

A litigious approach, with each client relying on partisan advice from their chosen lawyer in their own jurisdiction, can lead to a wide range of outcomes. The difference in outcome that would be imposed by one jurisdiction over another can at times be stark (and of course there is no substitute for careful advice on this).

But by choosing professionals who are familiar with and have a preference for an ADR process, and by using interest-based negotiations, clients can work towards a settlement which is outside what either jurisdiction would regard as the norm but which works for the whole family in a way which will feel acceptable to each client. International practitioners thus become familiar with e.g. the mid-Atlantic settlement, reflecting points of principle and law from both a US state and England and Wales which have been applied creatively.

13.4 TIME AND COST

To have a court-led dispute, on the other hand, about forum can be astoundingly time-consuming, expensive and damaging to the longer-term interests of a client, even if they were to 'win' the preliminary battle.

Skilled collaborative law practitioners can agree with their clients at an early stage to park the issue of forum whilst exploring an interest-based approach in the first place. Quite often feeding advice about forum into the process in a sensitive and sophisticated way will in fact empower the client with the stronger perceived position on forum to make concessions and move in a constructive way towards a negotiated outcome.

In any event using an ADR process is greatly preferable in terms of grounding the clients and reality-checking the extent to which they wish to dedicate months or years of their life arguing about where to argue, or if in fact both of them would prefer to move on.

We turn now to some of the specific issues and challenges that arise in the context of using ADR in international cases.

13.5 CAN ISSUING A PROTECTIVE WRIT BE CONSISTENT WITH ADR?

Experienced practitioners differ on the answer to this question, and healthy debate amongst collaborative law practitioners is in itself useful for placing into context the principles of ADR in international cases. The ADR committee of Resolution takes the view that in cases where an ADR process is being actively considered as an option for resolving issues pertaining to divorce, or indeed where an ADR course has already been committed to, it is preferable to avoid the pre-emptive issuing of suit proceedings to secure jurisdiction, because to do so goes against the whole ethos of ADR processes. Further, the view is taken that with advice given in a careful and clear way, and followed up in writing, including setting that advice in the context of the benefits to the client and their family as a whole of taking a non-confrontational approach, it will frequently be possible to empower the client into making an informed decision not to issue, but in a way which leaves the practitioner sufficiently protected from a negligence claim. What is imperative is that clients are able to make informed decisions and not have their lawyers make those decisions for them for fear of a negligence action. As such, issuing proceedings should be regarded as an option for discussion after collaborative law or mediation has been committed to, not as a precursor to negotiation.

The Resolution ADR committee is also mindful that there will be cases where the balance of risk/reward militates in favour of issuing proceedings as a first step, but that in this situation there remains scope for a collaborative law or collaborative law-based approach going forward. However, there is a risk that in these circumstances trust issues will arise between the parties and their respective legal teams which may then overshadow discussions going forward and threaten to derail the whole process.

13.6 COLLABORATIVE PARTICIPATION AGREEMENTS IN INTERNATIONAL CASES

As set out above, if the client decides to proceed with the collaborative law process without issuing proceedings in order to secure jurisdiction, it is strongly recommended that the practitioner confirms their advice in writing (including highlighting the fact that the spouse could decide to issue themselves and thereby gain an advantage); and that the client be asked to provide an indemnity that, notwithstanding that advice, he or she wishes to proceed with constructive discussions without issuing first with a view to signing a collaborative participation agreement. It is suggested that clients should be warned that the fact that their spouse has signed a collaborative participation agreement in itself would be very unlikely to prevent them pursuing proceedings in a foreign jurisdiction.

Neither solicitor who has signed a participation agreement can issue proceedings in England and Wales including a petition for divorce (or judicial separation) save with the consent of the other solicitor and their client. Consider, however, what is the position of the foreign lawyer? In England and Wales, collaborative lawyers should only collaborate with others who are members of Resolution, and failure to abide by their conduct rules could lead to them being barred. What would be the sanctions, if any, for a lawyer in another country?

Practitioners are also urged to distinguish between Brussells II and non-EU cases; inevitably in a Brussells II case the risk associated with not taking pre-emptive action, from the practitioner's point of view, is higher.

13.7 USE OF AN AGREED MORATORIUM

Many practitioners take the view that if both spouses wish to agree a moratorium or stay of proceedings in whichever jurisdiction they have been initiated, then there is nothing to prevent a collaborative participation agreement following, which bars either client from re-igniting any proceedings with their collaborative lawyer. It may be possible to issue a petition on anodyne grounds and then discuss with your possible future collaborative colleague the fact that the petition has been issued, what it contains, and why it was issued, with a view to an open discussion about whether a collaborative law process can still be followed and on what terms.

Some of the issues that need to be considered in this context include:

1. Is issuing proceedings and offering a moratorium likely, in practice, to move discussions in the direction of round-table negotiations rather than a proper collaborative case?
2. Would it be appropriate for the issuing party's lawyer to engage in future collaborative discussions?
3. Consider the reality of working with a collaborative practitioner in another jurisdiction, whose understanding of the collaborative law process may be different from your own, and who may not be subject to the same sanctions for breaking the terms or spirit of a collaborative participation agreement. Whose participation agreement is to be used? Can any guidance be derived from e.g. the Ethical Standards published by the International Academy of Collaborative Professionals? Is there a need for a protocol covering cross-border collaborative work involving Brussels II countries (presently being actively considered)?
4. Consider issues of payment of fees, location for four-way meetings, standardisation of documents, translations and enforcement.
5. Consider obtaining joint advice in a different jurisdiction, in order that collaborative lawyers can tell their respective clients of the merits of both jurisdictions for settlement purposes.
6. Particularly if you are in a jurisdiction which is less favourable to your client, and your client has taken the decision not to issue despite being entitled to do so, then consider very carefully obtaining a written waiver from your client to cover the situation where the other spouse ends the collaborative process and issues a petition in the forum most advantageous for them. Consider carefully the validity of the indemnity in any future proceedings for negligence, particularly in larger money cases. Consider taking advice as to whether it is likely to be enforceable.

13.8 SUMMARY

Without doubt any family lawyer taking on an international case needs to give extremely careful advice at the outset, recorded in writing, because of the potentially wide range of outcomes for the client in different jurisdictions. For the confident practitioner, however, this should be set in the context of the benefits for the client's wider and longer-term interests of pursuing from the outset an interest-based and problem-solving approach, rather than a confrontational one. Fear, on the part of the practitioner thinking of their indemnity policy, or on the part of the client that their spouse might steal a march, is a currency that all too often drives a process. As we know, it is fear that leads to misunderstandings, poor communication, and which can all too often fan the flames of conflict for a separating couple. In international cases, as with the subject matter covered in other sections of this book, there is scope for using the ADR skills we have acquired through mediating and collaborating to minimise the part of fear in the decision-making process, and to empower clients to choose the right process for them. Frequently, it is suggested, this will be to incorporate the benefits of ADR, even if it means the client's first step is an act of trust where it seems counter-intuitive to be doing so. We know they will thank us for helping them keep a balanced perspective when they most needed it.

CHAPTER 14

Privilege

Jonathan Southgate

Privilege arises in carefully defined yet not moribund categories of circumstances where a competing public interest has been recognised by the courts or the legislature to outweigh the general public interest that all relevant information should be disclosed to the court when determining disputes. It therefore acts to deny the court access to what would otherwise be relevant – and often highly relevant – material, including facts.

Privilege has been identified as a problem area for those practising alternative dispute resolution (ADR). Whilst traditional inter-lawyer negotiations are understood to be generally covered by without prejudice privilege, there has been less clarity concerning the privilege attaching to mediation and even less in the newer area of collaborative law, which is in many ways a hybrid between traditional inter-lawyer negotiations and mediation.

14.1 WITHOUT PREJUDICE PRIVILEGE

The public interest supporting without prejudice privilege is that parties should be encouraged to settle their disputes out of court through negotiation. In furtherance of that, it is recognised that, for negotiations to prove most effective, the participants should be unguarded and free to make concessions and admissions without fear that those concessions and admissions will subsequently be used against them outside the negotiation.

A second justification for without prejudice privilege is said to be the implied agreement between the participants that they will not seek to disclose their without prejudice communications to the court. However, it is clear that mere confidentiality is not of itself a category of privilege justifying non-disclosure from the court notwithstanding that breach of confidentiality may be actionable and capable of enforcement by injunction as against any party who seeks to publish confidential information.

14.1.2 Exceptions to without prejudice privilege

Whilst privilege arises as an exception to the general rule in favour of disclosure, it is also subject to its own exceptions. These can be viewed either as exceptions to the primary exception or instances where the primary exception does not arise. In the case of without prejudice privilege, the recognised exceptions are perhaps most helpfully set out in *Unilever Plc* v. *Procter & Gamble Co.* [1999] EWCA Civ 3027, [2000] 1 WLR 2436. Most pertinently, the exceptions permit (or do not prevent) the admissibility of evidence:

(a) as to whether a concluded agreement has been reached or whether an estoppel arises notwithstanding the absence of a concluded agreement;
(b) as to whether an agreement was based on misrepresentation, fraud or undue influence;
(c) of acts of *unambiguous impropriety* (see below);
(d) where the parties agree expressly or by implication to waive privilege.

Unambiguous impropriety

The scope of the 'unambiguous impropriety' exception has caused some difficulties but the court has increasingly emphasised that the exception is a narrow one. It is now clear that advancing an open position that is factually inconsistent with a statement made in without prejudice negotiations (such that perjury may be alleged) is not of itself enough. To come within the exception, the impropriety must be such that the privilege itself is clearly being abused (see *Savings & Investment Bank Ltd* v. *Fincken* [2003] EWCA Civ 1630, [2004] 1 All ER 1125). This approach strengthens the privilege considerably.

14.2 CIVIL MEDIATION

The legal framework of civil mediation is essentially contractual. The mediation agreement will commonly contain confidentiality agreements. Breach of the confidentiality agreement is actionable so that should one party seek to make disclosure to a third party in breach of the confidentiality agreement the court may enforce the agreement by granting an injunction.

However, as is discussed below, there is at present no recognised freestanding mediation privilege in English civil law. The privilege attaching to discussions during mediation is 'without prejudice' privilege. Indeed, most ADR is a form of assisted without prejudice negotiation.

14.3 CONCILIATION PRIVILEGE IN FAMILY LAW

The question of a separate category of mediation privilege applicable to family cases has been the subject of some judicial consideration. In *D* v. *National Society for the Prevention of Cruelty to Children* [1978] AC 171, at 226G, Lord Hailsham expressed the opinion that from the long-recognised category of without prejudice privilege a new category of privilege had developed based on public interest in the 'stability of marriage'. Similarly (at 236G) Lord Simon said that:

> With increasingly facile divorce and a vast rise in the number of broken marriages, with their concomitant penury and demoralisation, it came to be realised in the words of Bucknill LJ in *Mole* v. *Mole* at p23 that: 'in matrimonial disputes the state is also an interested party: it is more interested in reconciliation than in divorce'.
>
> This was the public interest which led to an application by analogy of the privilege of without prejudice communications to cover communications made in the course of matrimonial conciliation (see *McTaggart* v. *McTaggart* [1949] P 94, per Cohen LJ, at p.96, Denning LJ, at p.97; Denning LJ in *Mole* v. *Mole* [1951] P 21, 24; *Theodoropoulas* v. *Theodoropoulas* [1964] P 311) – so indubitably an extension of the law that the textbooks treat it as a separate category of relevant evidence that may be withheld from the court. It cannot be classified, like traditional without prejudice communications, as a privilege in aid of litigation.

The matter was considered further by the Court of Appeal in the context of proceedings under the Children Act 1989 in *Re D (Minors) (Conciliation: Privilege)* [1993] Fam 231, [1993] 1 FLR 932 in which Sir Thomas Bingham MR, whilst declining to debate its precise relationship with without prejudice privilege, recognised a separate head of privilege in disputes concerning children. Charting the growth of conciliation in children cases, Sir Thomas Bingham MR explicitly recognised, at 937H, that:

> Resolution of disputes over children by parents locked in acrimony and controversy has gradually but perceptibly taken over from efforts to preserve the state of the marriage of the parents.

Importantly, he thereby justified a shift in the public policy underlying the privilege from one of saving marriages to one of resolving conflict in disputes between parents concerning their children.

The Court of Appeal held that statements made in the course of meetings or communications made for the purpose of conciliation were not admissible save in the very unusual case where a statement had been made clearly indicating that the maker had in the past caused or was likely to cause serious harm to the well-being of a child. However, the decision was deliberately hedged by the further statement that: 'we have deliberately stated the law in terms appropriate to cover this case and no other'.

In *Unilever Plc* v. *Procter & Gamble Co.* [1999] EWCA Civ 3027, referring to *Re D* during his discussion of without prejudice privilege, Robert Walker LJ described this privilege as a 'hybrid species'.

The President's Direction dated 25 May 2000 concerning ancillary relief procedure [2000] 1 FLR 2000 provides in relation to financial dispute resolution (FDR) appointments that:

> Such meetings which were previously described as meetings held for the purposes of conciliation have been developed as a means of reducing the tension which inevitably arises in matrimonial and family disputes and facilitating settlement of those disputes . . .
>
> In order for the FDR appointment to be effective, parties must approach the occasion openly and without reserve. Non-disclosure of the content of such meetings is accordingly vital and is an essential prerequisite for fruitful discussion directed to the settlement of the dispute between the parties. The FDR appointment is an important part of the settlement process. As a consequence of *Re D (Minors)(Conciliation: Disclosure of Information)* [1993] Fam 231; *sub nom Re D (Minors)(Conciliation: Privilege)* [1993] 1 FLR 932, evidence of anything said or of any admission made in the course of an FDR appointment will not be admissible in evidence, except at the trial of a person for an offence committed at the appointment or in the very exceptional circumstances indicated in *Re D.*

A consequence of the Practice Direction has been that ancillary relief negotiations leading up to and following an FDR appointment have routinely been conducted on a without prejudice basis, subject to the exceptions thereto, whereas the FDR appointment itself has been at least formally treated as having a higher degree of privilege almost without relevant exception. Until the new costs rules abolished the admissibility of *Calderbank* offers on the question of costs in ancillary relief proceedings, it was the case that, whilst the *Calderbank* material could be routinely admitted and debated during the FDR process, anything said during the FDR itself could not be referred to in any subsequent *Calderbank* letter which it was intended later to put before the court on the question of costs.

There has as yet been no direct challenge mounted to the application by the President of *Re D* conciliation privilege to FDRs, but were a party to be guilty of, for example, an act of fraud or unambiguous impropriety which amounted to an abuse of the privilege, then it is, in the view of the author, likely that the court would find it very difficult to avoid piercing the privilege in order to achieve fairness between the parties to the negotiations.

Indeed in *Rose* v. *Rose (Divorce: Consent Orders) (No. 1)* [2002] EWCA Civ 208, [2002] 1 FLR 978, the Court of Appeal appears to have had no compunction about conducting a complete survey of an FDR hearing with the benefit of a full transcript in order to determine whether the husband should be bound by the approved agreement arising from it. This is in line with the exceptions to without prejudice privilege but not *Re D* privilege. It seems that the privilege point may not have been taken.

In *I* v. *I* [2008] EWHC 1167 (Fam), [2009] 1 FLR 201, it appears that Charles J formed the view that he could consider the FDR material in order to decide an issue of non-disclosure, although the point does not appear to have been argued to the hilt and/or given full judicial consideration. However, on appeal, the decision of Charles J to consider the FDR material was questioned by the Court of Appeal. Whilst explicitly stating that the decision of Charles J was not to be followed, the Court of Appeal studiedly chose to express no positive view on the topic: *Bokor-Ingram* v. *Bokor-Ingram* [2009] EWCA Civ 412, [2009] 2 FLR 922.

In *Myerson* v. *Myerson* [2008] EWCA Civ 1376, [2009] 1 FLR 826 the question arose as to the extent to which a judge could deal with directions and other matters subsequent to dealing with the FDR and within the context of the prohibition on such further involvement provided by r.2.61E(2) of the Family Proceedings Rules 1991, SI 1991/1247. In his judgment, Thorpe LJ stated that the underlying policy of the subrule was to guarantee distrustful and anxious litigants the same degree of confidentiality at an FDR as they would enjoy had the case been referred to an outside mediation professional and that it was therefore important that the FDR judge should have no further involvement save for approving a consent order, helping to resolve peripheral issues as to the precise terms or language by which the order is to be expressed, conducting another FDR or giving directions for trial.

In his judgment, Lawrence Collins LJ went outside the remit of the appeal to suggest that the parties might agree to waive the prohibition against the further involvement of the FDR judge in their case and that such a waiver would not undermine the public policy of encouraging settlement or protecting without prejudice communications. Thorpe and Goldring LJJ declined to express a view on the waiver topic. Whether the views of Lawrence Collins LJ will prevail and if so extend to the question of the potential waiver of the prohibition on admitting FDR material is perhaps a speculation too far. Plainly, in the Family Division, privilege is an area which the Court of Appeal is actively considering with the importance of ADR firmly in mind.

14.4 A SEPARATE CATEGORY OF MEDIATION PRIVILEGE?

In *Brown* v. *Rice* [2007] EWHC 625 (Ch), a case well publicised amongst ADR practitioners, Stuart Isaacs QC sitting as a deputy judge of the High Court was invited to consider the authorities on family conciliation privilege and whether a distinct privilege separate from without prejudice privilege could be recognised across all forms of mediation, i.e. a distinct category of mediation privilege. The ADR Group were given leave to intervene. The case concerned a mediation conducted at solicitors' offices involving the parties and their solicitors and conducted by a mediator subject to the terms of a fairly standard mediation agreement containing blanket confidentiality clauses and a clause to the effect that no binding agreement could arise until it had been reduced to writing and signed. Having considered the authorities, the deputy judge held that:

- mediation is a form of assisted without prejudice negotiation;
- the confidentiality clauses 'bolster' the without prejudice privilege but could not be treated as absolute and could not prevent:

  - the court from looking at documents produced at the mediation which had been created for other purposes; or
  - the court from hearing evidence pursuant to one of the generally recognised exceptions to the without prejudice rule as to whether an agreement had been reached; and
- the clause in the mediation agreement to the effect that no agreement would be binding unless reduced to writing and signed did not prevent the court from hearing evidence as to the question of whether it had been waived during the mediation.

Whilst recognising the line of authority based on *D* v. *National Society for the Prevention of Cruelty to Children* and *Re D*, the deputy judge said that he did not himself find support for a distinct category of mediation privilege but did say at [20]:

> It may be in the future that the existence of a distinct mediation privilege will require to be considered by either the legislature or the courts but that is not something that arises for decision now.

He was able to proceed as he did to his conclusions on the basis of a concession by the parties that the case before him could be decided under the without prejudice rule.

14.5 EU LEGISLATION

There is in existence an EU Mediation Directive (2008/52/EC) adopted by the European Parliament on 24 April 2008 and published in the Official Journal on 21 May 2008. By article 12, EU member states must implement the provisions within three years, i.e. by 21 May 2011. The EU Directive caters for mediation in transnational or cross-border disputes (i.e. disputes between parties habitually resident or domiciled in different member states). However, member states may choose to apply its provisions to purely domestic disputes. This represents an opportunity for the UK government to express its commitment to mediation and to enhance participation in mediation within the UK.

An aim of the Directive would appear to be to provide a stable and predictable legal framework for mediation in a balanced relationship with judicial proceedings and in that context to ensure, amongst other things, access and recourse to mediation, the quality of mediation and the enforceability of agreements reached through mediation.

Article 7 of the Directive deals with confidentiality of mediation and provides that:

> . . . member states shall ensure that, unless the parties agree otherwise, neither mediators nor those involved in the administration of the mediation process shall be compelled to give evidence in civil and commercial judicial proceedings or

arbitration regarding information out of or in connection with a mediation process, except:

(a) where this is necessary for overriding considerations of public policy of the Member State concerned, in particular when required to ensure the protection of the best interests of children or to prevent harm to the physical or psychological integrity of a person; or
(b) where disclosure of the content of the agreement resulting from mediation is necessary in order to implement or enforce that agreement.

The scope of these confidentiality provisions is potentially wide enough to encompass some or all of the exceptions to the existing without prejudice rule on public policy grounds.

14.6 CONCLUSIONS

Drawing these strands together it seems that:

- The courts are highly supportive of ADR and are in general likely to uphold confidentiality clauses where one party seeks to reveal outside the ADR process matters which they have agreed should be kept confidential.
- However, save in the case of family conciliation, the only recognised form of privilege attaching to ADR is without prejudice privilege to which the recognised limited exceptions continue to apply notwithstanding the terms of any confidentiality clauses.
- Family conciliation privilege is a separate category of privilege attaching to conciliation concerning children.
- As things stand, as a result of the President's Direction, family conciliation privilege also covers FDR appointments but it may well be that the court would in practice apply some or all of the general exceptions applicable to without prejudice privilege in order to achieve fairness between the parties.
- Whilst there is at present no recognised mediation privilege applicable to all forms of mediation in the broad sense, the existence of the EU Mediation Directive presents the UK government with the opportunity to provide a single coherent legal framework for mediation, including as to privilege and confidentiality.

The ADR committee of Resolution is in the process of drawing up guidance as to best practice for ADR practitioners regarding the approach to be taken to matters of privilege with a view to avoiding or at least reducing the risk and incidence of questions of privilege in family ADR being litigated in the courts.

CHAPTER 15

Support structures

Sarah Lloyd and Kim Beatson

The role of the family lawyer is changing. Mediators and collaborative lawyers are working with clients in new and innovative ways and lawyers are encountering situations which present them with very different challenges from those they face in traditional practice. Many are recognising that they will be better equipped to work with their clients if they acquire and have experience of using a variety of different skills in addition to those they already use. Mediation, collaborative law and other training can provide family lawyers with additional skills for them to use with their clients both within these processes and inevitably outside them too.

15.1 THE NEED FOR SUPPORT

Would family lawyers working with clients within these different processes find support for this work helpful? Most professionals will derive some benefit from receiving support, feedback or supervision either from their peers or from more experienced members of their chosen profession in the exercise of their daily professional lives. Many professional organisations have already recognised this and require their members to show that they have such support or supervision in place. Others are waking up to its benefits. Since the early 1980s solicitors have been required by their professional body, the Law Society of England and Wales, to obtain a certain amount of annual approved training. Now, included within the definition of that approved training is the possibility of receiving mentoring or other professional supervision or support. Family lawyers work increasingly alongside other professionals from different backgrounds in an effort to provide appropriate expertise to assist clients in resolving their disputes. As a result, family lawyers are becoming more aware of the support and assistance available to other professionals and some are questioning whether it would be helpful to introduce a more formal support structure into their own practice.

Many professions have devised ways of providing support for their members. In some cases this will mean little or no formal support; in others such support will be compulsory. No therapist would dream of working without supervision and support, nor would they be allowed to work without it. In the therapy world supervision is understood by all professionals to be a vital and necessary part of their practice and is compulsory. At the moment supervision is not part of the culture for lawyers. Once their training is over and they are qualified they frequently have little formal supervision of their work and rarely have the opportunity to obtain support from a more experienced colleague. There are few opportunities to stand back from the day job and look at the wider picture. Though most lawyers will be able to remember a moment in their career when they would have benefited from support from someone with more experience, they may also remember that there were few options available to them when this happened. There are few experienced lawyers whose office door is open to the less experienced lawyer. In difficult economic times it is likely that such support barely exists. Paradoxically though, this is probably the time when wise counsel would be even more useful. Despite this it continues to be hard to find.

Many lawyers will obtain some support on an informal basis from their peers. The lucky ones will have access within the partnership/company for which they work to a more formal structure offering some form of support or mentoring. The annual appraisal may also provide a rare opportunity to obtain or at least request support. For the lucky few some more formal support in their practice is available.

15.2 WHAT DO WE MEAN BY SUPPORT STRUCTURES?

This chapter aims to provide a brief explanation of a number of different support services available to lawyers generally as well as those available specifically to members of Resolution and then covers in more depth those set up to be of assistance to lawyers trained in and offering alternative methods of dispute resolution such as mediation and the collaborative law process and is specifically focused on these areas.

15.3 INFORMAL SUPPORT

Support may be informal and unstructured or formal and structured and will typically consist of a mixture of both. The range of less formal and structured support for lawyers might start with the giving of guidance and assistance in their daily work such as checking advice before it is given to clients, reviewing and amending letters, which might be particularly helpful to more junior lawyers but which lawyers of all levels of experience will welcome from time to time. At the other end of the spectrum support might include help with dealing with difficult clients, work colleagues and personal problems.

Most lawyers will also benefit from informal feedback from work colleagues and in an ideal world would be both receiving this for themselves and providing it to others. Such support will include occasions when a colleague pops in to another colleague's office to 'just run something by you'. Often a specific person in the firm will be sought out for reassurance on a particular query because they are known for having dealt with that situation or a similar one before. Sometimes a specific person is regularly the one to whom queries are addressed because they are known in the firm for having a welcoming, sympathetic and open manner. However, generally such support or reassurance is being offered in relation only to client issues.

A more structured approach may exist within some firms and this might cover some of the above, may include a regular team meeting and there may be a formal support process and even a mentoring scheme. Some employers may offer access to a confidential counselling service. Where a mentoring scheme is in place it is likely that the structure will be more formal.

15.4 EXISTING FORMAL SUPPORT AND MENTORING SCHEMES

15.4.1 The Law Society of England and Wales

The Law Society of England and Wales offers help and support for solicitors who find themselves in a difficult situation and seek support. The Law Society website provides links to organisations which offer free and confidential support with both personal and professional problems for solicitors in England and Wales (**www.lawsociety.org.uk**). A whole range of potential areas of difficulty is listed with details of how to obtain further information and help including support groups covering addiction, bullying, debt, depression, discrimination, employment, ethics, finance, practice management and stress.

15.4.2 Association of Women Solicitors

The Association of Women Solicitors (AWS) runs a mentoring scheme for its members for work-related issues where it defines mentoring as 'a one-to-one non-judgmental relationship in which an individual (the mentor) voluntarily gives of his/her time to support, advise or encourage another person (the mentee)'. Helpfully, the scheme details make it clear what is and what is not covered and identify the most common areas that cause mentees to contact a mentor under their scheme: changing specialism, moving from or to private practice from an in-house position, moving to another area of the country, flexible working, combining career and family, returning to the profession after a career break, thinking of applying for a promotion or judicial appointment. The scheme does not provide legal advice on the matters raised or offer work experience or training contracts. It does not deal with medical issues such as depression or with forms of psychological counselling (**www.womensolicitors.org.uk**).

Mentees who are considering any of these issues can be put in touch with lawyers who have already faced these situations and can advise from experience. There is an opportunity to have two separate conversations with the mentor who offers constructive advice gained from their own professional experience. Mentees have reported that the scheme has encouraged them and boosted their confidence. The mentors give their time on a voluntary basis, and aim to listen and to offer constructive advice gained from their own professional experience. To access the scheme prospective mentees fill out a form setting out their query and they are then matched to a mentor who contacts them direct. They have an initial conversation which could last up to one hour with the possibility of a follow-up call if they wish. Many mentors have expressed satisfaction in being able to give something back to others in the profession.

15.4.3 Resolution

Resolution also offers a mentoring scheme for its members. The scheme was initially launched at the annual conference in 2003. Resolution allocated some of its resources to train a number of its more experienced members to take on the role of a mentor. Resolution Mentoring is a confidential resource for all members. It creates a forum for them to discuss work-related issues or problems with people who understand very well the pressures of life in practice as a busy family lawyer. The system was re-launched at the 2008 Resolution conference in Brighton accompanied by a cartoon campaign which regularly appears in the Resolution journal, *Review*. There is further information on the Resolution website (**www.resolution.org.uk**).

Resolution mentors are available to discuss any difficulties the member may be experiencing with clients or colleagues. They are solicitors who understand the pressures of life in practice and have been specially trained by Resolution to provide this service.

Resolution members wishing to use this scheme may select a mentor who is local to them or one they never come across professionally. The mentor can give 40 minutes of their time to the mentee on one or two occasions. In that time they can help to formulate a strategy to ease the stress. All the mentors have undergone an intensive two-day mentoring training programme.

The organisation maintains a list of mentors and the prospective mentee can choose and make contact with one of the mentors on the list – using a pseudonym if they wish. They will not be asked for their name or firm. The mentor will ask for and make a note of the age of the mentee within a band, gender, year of qualification, broad geographic region and broad outline of the problem for evaluation purposes.

The scheme is completely confidential (save in instances where allegations of child abuse or money laundering are raised). The mentor will not retain notes of the session.

15.5 SUPPORT STRUCTURES SPECIFICALLY FOR RESOLUTION MEDIATORS

The authors of the mediation foundation training course for Resolution recognised the need for a support structure for lawyers working as mediators to be built into the ongoing requirements for mediators after successful completion of the training. Family lawyers are used to dealing primarily with legal issues arising upon separation and divorce. Other forms of dispute resolution require the use of different skills which are introduced and practised during the mediation training. Most lawyers will find, at some stage, that working as a mediator will take them outside their comfort zone. Support structures can offer help and guidance to lawyer mediators who are dealing with issues and emotions which they may not have had to address before.

15.5.1 Buddy groups

Resolution-trained mediators are encouraged on the training to form *buddy* groups with their local mediator colleagues and to meet on a regular basis in order to get to know each other and to share concerns in a safe and confidential environment. Getting to know other local mediators better is a proven way of increasing mediation practice as it is often the case that lawyers will refer to a mediator they know rather than to one they do not. Referral to mediation by a lawyer who understands the mediation process can have huge benefits for the clients and may assist in leading to a successful outcome. The form and content of the group meetings is not prescribed. Many of these groups work on marketing their mediation services locally to the possible users, the courts and other potential referrers and on making the local media aware of their existence by speaking on local radio, writing articles for regional and local newspapers and other publications. Some invest in a leaflet to market their services and themselves as mediators. Resolution provides its mediators with a marketing pack to assist them with promotion of the process together with an options leaflet and a leaflet specifically explaining the mediation process. Groups also meet to discuss practice issues and difficulties experienced in their local area. Whilst it is strongly encouraged that mediators meet in this way, some mediators work in isolated areas where owing to the scarcity of mediators, no local group exists and where this would not be possible. For this reason membership of a buddy group whilst strongly encouraged cannot be compulsory.

15.5.2 Professional practice consultant

To comply with Resolution and Family Mediation Council requirements, all mediators must have a professional practice consultant (PPC) who oversees their work and to whom they may refer if they experience any problems and to discuss their work generally. Some people refer to them as 'supervisors'. Many of the unfamiliar situations mediators can encounter during the course of their work can be discussed with their PPC and strategies for dealing with these situations can be considered together.

The PPC is appointed shortly after the mediator has successfully completed the mediation foundation training course. A PPC is an experienced mediator who has undergone a further training course to learn how to supervise mediators. All Resolution mediators must undergo a minimum of 12 hours of supervision from their PPC and peer group meetings in the first two years (of which at least four hours should be PPC consultancy) after completing the course and they should certify to that effect on an ongoing annual basis when they complete their return and submit their annual subscription to Resolution. There is also an accreditation scheme. Mediators who have public funded contracts have different requirements set down by the Legal Services Commission (see LSC QMS at **www.lsc.gov.org**).

Sometimes buddy group meetings are combined with supervision sessions from the PPC and it is very common for PPCs to meet with a number of mediators together over a half day and for there to be both group and individual supervision during that time. Mediators will book an individual session with the PPC in advance.

In addition PPCs can be available over the phone for support when needed to help to deal with individual concerns or matters arising in mediation cases in between supervision sessions. Should the designated PPC not be available on the phone then there is a helpline number which Resolution mediators can use where such help and assistance is urgently required.

PPCs have a responsibility to oversee the work of newly trained mediators (some may offer to co-mediate with newly trained mediators in order to give them both some experience and confidence before launching themselves as a sole mediator). PPCs will review case summaries of the first few mediations conducted by a newly trained mediator before they are sent out to clients and will spend time debriefing the mediation sessions with their consultee mediators and addressing any difficulties and concerns. They will assist in identifying ongoing training needs and in some instances provide training as part of the consultation process. Where mediators are applying for mediation accreditation they will do so only when their PPC judges that they have sufficient experience. The PPC will review the accreditation portfolio and provide a confidential report on the mediator's practice which the PPC sends to the accreditation panel in support of the application. The PPC's report carries considerable weight and is a highly influential document in the accreditation process.

15.5.3 Training days and conferences

Ongoing training days and conferences also contribute in an ad hoc fashion to the mediators' support structure as they provide the opportunity for mediators from different mediation fields to meet and exchange ideas and views and obtain some validation for what they do. These opportunities for support are extremely important for the more isolated mediator although, of course, the job of a mediator is by its very nature an isolated one. When working as a mediator there is no one else in the room to observe the way in which the mediator handles the mediation and no one to offer feedback on the mediator's performance.

15.5.4 Observation of a mediator's practice

There has been much debate over the years between the different mediation organisations as to whether the PPC (or other suitably qualified experienced mediator) should undertake direct observation of a mediator's practice. Whilst there are advantages to this form of supervision, particularly from the point of view of quality control, there are a number of potential difficulties not least the fact that the couple involved in the mediation may not be willing to allow another person to be in the room and observe the mediation. Even if the couple are prepared to allow observation of the mediation, there is the risk that the presence of another person may render the mediation process less comfortable for the couple and may alter the dynamics. If the mediation subsequently breaks down the couple may attribute the breakdown of the process to the presence of a third party at a crucial moment.

15.5.5 Why have structured supervision for mediators?

One of the main reasons why the structured supervision framework within which mediators must work was set up was to address the difficulties caused by the isolated nature of the work mediators do. It was also strongly influenced by the supervision structure set up for non-lawyer mediators coming from a therapeutic background. As the supervision structure was already an integrated part of a therapist's practice, this structure was incorporated into their work as mediators. The Family Mediators' Association (FMA) was established around 25 years ago and devised a family mediation training course for mediators both from a legal background and from a therapeutic background where both were trained together. FMA training was initially in a co-mediation model only, where a lawyer mediator and a mediator from a therapeutic background would mediate together. Both the lawyer mediator and the non-lawyer mediator would be chosen for their specific area of expertise giving careful consideration to the particular needs of the clients. This has now changed and training is in both sole and co-mediation. The Resolution training model, which owes much to the FMA original (not least because at least one of the authors of the course also wrote the Resolution training) has, from the beginning, offered training in a sole mediation model but with reference to a co-mediation model.

15.6 SUPPORT STRUCTURES SPECIFICALLY FOR RESOLUTION COLLABORATIVE LAWYERS

Collaborative law practice is substantially different from traditional legal practice as well as from other ADR models, and presents specific challenges not necessarily addressed by the ethical standards of individual disciplines.

It has previously been observed that working within other dispute resolution processes can take lawyers away from their traditional roles and into uncharted waters. Lawyers working within the collaborative law process will find themselves facing situations that they have hitherto not encountered, as it is common for issues to arise which are not strictly of a legal nature. These may be situations which require a commonsense approach, or situations which require the employment of a different style or strategy from the manner in which the lawyer might traditionally have addressed it. The training which every collaborative lawyer within this jurisdiction must undergo will assist lawyers by providing them with specific skills and strategies to use. Sometimes the parties will require a more specialist intervention. But the dynamics of a process where both parties are present in the room together with their lawyers are different, so dealing with these situations will challenge lawyers in a different way from the challenges they have previously encountered in the traditional process. The collaborative lawyer who is also a practising mediator will in addition notice a difference in the dynamic of the collaborative law process compared to mediation. At the most basic level this is inevitable because in family mediation the mediator is usually alone in the room with the mediating couple whereas in the collaborative process both the lawyers are present in the room with the couple.

Understandably, there may be a natural tendency for the collaborative lawyer to retreat back to the relatively safe haven and comfort zone that is the positional role in the negotiations when they encounter a difficult issue. This is even more likely to happen when the lawyers involved in a collaborative law process have not had an opportunity to get to know each other properly in advance of the start of the case. Although it is part of the collaborative law process that the lawyers should meet in advance of the start of a case to discuss the process and should continue to meet or communicate by phone to discuss issues and tactics for as long as the case continues, the level of trust which is required between the lawyers may need to be built up over a number of cases. The degree of trust which exists between the two collaborative lawyers has frequently been cited as being the single most important factor in the success or failure of a case. For this reason Resolution imposes an obligation upon all of its collaborative lawyers to join a POD or practice group. (POD stands for practice and organisational development group and aptly describes precisely the point of its creation. However the use of POD and practice group is interchangeable.)

15.6.1 The practice and organisational development group or POD

Practice groups are groups of like-minded individuals who meet periodically to discuss issues of common concern including training, practice problems, best practice, ethics and the development of practice and solutions.

Throughout the collaborative law world practice groups or PODs have varied between communities and jurisdictions.

In England and Wales the primary focus of PODs is best practice solutions and development of interdisciplinary working. In Illinois that is much the same. However, in Cincinnati the groups are very large. Meetings are divided into business meetings and meetings for training purposes.

15.6.2 Why are PODs so important?

The primary purpose of practice groups is to facilitate networking and to develop relationships of trust between members. This is fundamental to the collaborative process.

Establishing interdisciplinary practice groups is particularly important to that end, which is why many US states and UK PODs invite other family professionals such as financial neutrals and parenting coaches to attend practice group meetings. Many collaborative lawyers are also mediators and the POD may have the dual use in enabling dual-trained mediators/collaborative lawyers to discuss practice areas of relevance to both.

Mature PODs have gone much further and are able to offer the following:

- Printing advertisements/Powerpoint presentations and handouts for community speaking (Wisconsin).
- Developing members-only sections of the website (England and Wales).
- Coordinating the distribution of brochures/materials to referral sources (Massachusetts).
- Data collection by POD (and of course this may be undertaken by overarching bodies such as Resolution and IACP).
- Discussion groups and presentations by regional groups (New York).
- Collaborative retreats for members to renew energy (San Francisco).

When developing a practice group the following activities may be of interest:

- Social activities.
- Inviting other POD leaders to share initiatives.
- Training as a group.
- Group retreats.
- Study groups.
- Buddies or mentors.
- Encouraging applications to higher national boards such as the IACP board.

- Delegating speakers to inform the public – that could include local business centres or chambers of commerce, schools, universities.
- Writing articles as a means of publicity.

15.6.3 Where are the PODs?

PODs exist wherever there are a few trained collaborative lawyers. Resolution maintains a list of PODs on its website (**www.resolution.org.uk**).

15.6.4 How do you join one?

The first challenge for a freshly trained collaborative lawyer is to find a POD to join. In some communities this will be easy as there will only be one or two to choose from and these will welcome new members with open arms. In other communities where there are perhaps a number of large PODs it may be hard not only to find a POD which will accept you but also to decide which to apply to as PODs tend to develop along different lines, particularly where there are a number in the same densely populated area. London has faced some very specific challenges and has met these challenges head on. Sometimes the only solution is to form a new POD. Far from being the worst-case scenario this can often be exactly the right option, particularly where those forming a new POD have just completed their training together and are likely to be working together. They may already have gone some way to forming that bond of trust so crucial to the highest levels of collaborative practice.

The first port of call for any newly trained collaborative lawyer looking for a POD to join is to check on the Resolution website list of PODs to find out if there is one in their area and then to contact the POD liaison officer (PLO) to see whether that POD is willing to take on new members. Most are happy to have new members. Some PLOs may have contacted the newly trained collaborative lawyer first. A list of newly trained collaborative lawyers goes out by email to all PLOs and also appears in the Resolution newsletter *Alternative Enews* to which all Resolution ADR section members are automatically subscribed.

15.6.5 How big should a POD be?

Research on the international scene does not seem to indicate a prescriptive view on the size of the PODs. However, the need to establish a sense of trust and rhythm seems to indicate that benefits will be found in smaller groups. In Los Angeles and some parts of England and Wales subgroups have formed when POD numbers have rendered it unwieldy.

It is possible to join more than one POD in England and quite commonplace in large cities such as London where collaborative lawyers frequently join PODs local to home and to office.

London PODs have developed their role so that it now includes developing tools for educating clients about collaborative law and ADR, strategies for enrolling clients or their spouses, and how to effectively deal with four-way meetings.

Encouraging attendance at POD meetings is important. Continued enrolment as a collaborative lawyer is dependent upon the acquisition of professional development points.

15.6.6 Are there any POD rules?

It is up to individual PODs how they work but Resolution has produced a set of guidelines to assist newly forming PODs. See POD guidelines for good practice.

15.6.7 The role of the POD liaison officer

The role of the POD liaison officer (PLO) is informal by definition but involves chairing meetings, dealing with the administration of the POD and organising meetings, agendas, seminars and practice development. However, the PLO is an important link into Resolution head office and is the named person on the Resolution website where each POD is listed. PLOs are invited to two meetings every year by Resolution when important issues are discussed. This is a hugely important forum for discussion and a place where all POD members can have their concerns raised.

15.6.8 What you discuss at a POD meeting

The guidelines set out in general terms the remit of the POD meetings. It is vital that the members of a POD get an opportunity to discuss practice issues and this should be given priority. Many PODs arrange role plays in order to tackle common concerns and difficult situations which can arise within a collaborative law four-way meeting.

15.6.9 What PODs could do in addition to what they currently do

PODs will inevitably develop in different ways. Factors affecting the development of PODs may be geographical, cultural, numerical, whether based in rural or urban areas, the ratio of lawyers and other professionals, and the enthusiasm for the process in their local areas from other influences such as judges and courts generally.

PODs and individual POD members generally serve a useful purpose in supporting their members through a process which is frequently challenging the members in different ways. Some PODs in other jurisdictions have taken this further and set up a formal structure to offer support and help to members both during and after a case. Some practice groups organise debriefing sessions at the conclusion of a case so that all members of the team have an opportunity to discuss how they feel the case progressed. This also gives everyone a forum to discuss what it might be good to improve in terms of process or support.

Some groups have volunteer members who will offer to give some of their time for free (usually a couple of hours) to listen to individual concerns and in other groups a more formal system is in place.

One group in another jurisdiction has designed a facilitation process for specific issues to be addressed. There is a formal procedure for invoking that process including the requirement that all participants should sign a confidentiality contract prior to the start of the facilitation. The facilitation is led by one member of the group who was not involved in the particular case and all members of the team attend the facilitation meeting or meetings. The facilitator is chosen from those trained collaborative professionals within the group who have demonstrated their skills in applying collaborative principles and the skills of their own profession in completed collaborative cases. They may come from any of the professional groups represented within the POD. One member of a collaborative team may request this service and the facilitator will talk to all the parties involved individually before sitting down with all of them to discuss the issues raised. This process provides a safe and confidential place for collaborative professionals to address process issues, problems that develop in a specific collaborative case, or an issue or problem which develops between or among collaborative professionals. This model can provide assurance to the public that members of such a group will model and practise collaboratively at the highest level of their competence and integrity. This sort of model may well be one that other groups have adopted or may wish to consider offering to their members.

15.6.10 How members feel about their PODs

In many cases PODs have become mini communities. They provide a unique form of social and professional networking for collaborative family lawyers and other related professions. For most PODs the meeting is a mix of socialising and official business. Some make available wine and other refreshments. Some even hold their meetings in a wine bar or other public place. This emphasises the social nature of the groups. It is also clear that these groups provide a vital form of support and a safe haven for all professionals working in the collaborative process. In New Orleans in 2005 after the devastation caused by Hurricane Katrina POD members were keen to renew contact and meet up as soon as practicable. This helped them to recapture a sense of normality in their lives.

15.6.11 Should PODs police members?

What can PODs do to regulate the collaborative work of a POD member who, it is reported by other members, is not adhering to the rules or the spirit of the process? PODs are considering this and working out their own ways of coping with individual members who are reported by other members of the group as not behaving appropriately within the process.

From the above it is clear that the POD serves a vital role as the primary source of support for the collaborative lawyer and indeed for other professionals working within the collaborative field. It should be the first port of call for all practitioners seeking help, information and support. However, it is likely that in some instances a more confidential form of support may be required.

Although there is a requirement that newly trained collaborative lawyers join and remain members of a POD, there is no current rule requiring collaborative lawyers to have any form of supervision. This is currently under review. Anecdotally we hear that many collaborative lawyers who are also mediators are bringing collaborative issues to their meetings with their PPCs for discussion. As we have described above some PODs are setting up support structures for their members to use if required. It is possible that some PPCs could assist as mentors for collaborative lawyers where the PPC has collaborative training and/or experience either as a lawyer or as a family consultant. In this new field we must ensure that we continue to respond to the needs of the practitioners and continue to keep under review the way in which they are being supported. We will be continuing to look for other ways in which such support might be obtained both for collaborative lawyers and for mediators.

CHAPTER 16

What next?

Andrew Greensmith and Emma Harte

With the increasing number of early intervention court schemes, the re-launch of the Court of Appeal Family Mediation Scheme and the launch of a dedicated family mediation helpline, it is clear that the government and the judiciary increasingly see alternative dispute resolution (ADR) as being helpful to clients, helping better communication, reducing acrimony and costs, etc. and as such, it is becoming more widely encouraged.

The courts are making more information available to court users about options open to them and it is to be hoped that ADR will be seen as more mainstream and 'normal' rather than 'alternative'. The ideal we should aspire to is the system in Australia where, save in exceptional circumstances, court applications cannot proceed until such time as the various issues have been aired in mediation or some other alternative process and that process has failed or broken down.

In Australia, it appears that the alternatives to court have become mainstream and the court route is the alternative. It is not only in Australia that this is happening but in other places such as Hong Kong, Canada and certain states of the US. Many family lawyers worldwide are choosing not to litigate: their practices consist solely of mediation, collaborative law and cooperative work where court is avoided. An example of someone who has done exactly that is a family law specialist from California, Forrest ('Woody') Mosten. He argues that it is difficult to be both a good advocate and a good mediator and collaborative law practitioner, and now has what he calls a 'peacemaking practice'. He realised that clients wanted solutions to their problems, and did not necessarily need to be going down the court route to achieve that.

The statistics support his case. Recent studies have found that in California almost 70 per cent of family law litigants do not have a lawyer on either side of the court case when the matter is filed, and that percentage increases to 80 per cent by the time the matter is finalised.

Those litigants who do engage lawyers might just want initial advice, a second opinion, or proposals to put forward in mediation. For Mosten, this is probably the future for family lawyers. Clients do not necessarily want lawyers to do all the work and do not need 'all the trimmings', so we should be prepared to offer just what they require. We would need to set out clear boundaries and responsibilities, and should advertise and be clear about what we offer. This would include building our offices to show clients that they are at the centre of our work by having, for example, a dedicated client office with a library and computer which could also double up as another waiting room.

Woody Mosten offers many tips on how to build a successful law practice, with clients at its centre, without ever going to court, and this is quite possibly the way forward in England and Wales. Not many clients can afford to go down the court route and those who can often wish to resolve matters privately and amicably. As Woody comments, litigators can be consulted where necessary in the mediation and collaborative law processes in order to help bring about settlement.

Not to be forgotten either is the role of family arbitration. Resolution has worked in collaboration with the Chartered Institute of Arbitrators, the Family Law Bar Association, the Law Society of England and Wales and other stakeholders to design a training and accreditation scheme for family arbitration. Other jurisdictions already have binding family arbitration and an eventual aim would be to have a change to primary legislation in England and Wales. This initiative is very much in its early stages, but has attracted support from some senior members of the judiciary. Until such time as arbitration is supported by legislation, however, it is intended that arbitrated awards will be considered by the courts to be as binding as *Edgar*-type agreements. For the present time, matters relating to the welfare of children will not be the subject of arbitration.

Given the privacy and speed arbitration will offer, it is hoped that this option will offer a viable alternative to the court process for some couples.

If alternatives to court are made more mainstream, it is clear that the role of the traditional family lawyer will change radically over the coming decades. If we look back at how family law – and Resolution – have evolved over the last 25 years (and even over the last 10 years), there has been an enormous shift in thinking and practices, with clients becoming far more knowledgeable, and, importantly, cost conscious. Given the changes worldwide, in Australia, etc., it looks like ADR will not be alternative at all but normal and mainstream. Furthermore, it is highly probable that peacemaking practices in the Woody Mosten model will be commonplace.

APPENDIX 1

Top 10 tips for mediators and collaborative practitioners

1. Prepare well

Preparation is critical before any mediation or collaborative meetings. As mediator or collaborative practitioner, you are managing the process and the clients are looking to you to take control.

You should therefore set agendas at the start of any mediation session or well before any collaborative four-way meetings with your fellow collaborative colleague. You should also review notes and minutes of previous sessions and meetings and when working collaboratively, speak with your collaborative colleague and your client before each meeting to make sure there are no surprises to be revealed suddenly and to try to iron out or predict any potential stumbling blocks.

2. Stay curious

This was a top tip given by Nancy Cameron, QC and President of the International Academy of Collaborative Practitioners at the Resolution Alternative Dispute Resolution Conference in July 2009. It is important to stay curious and to ask lots of questions as often the key to moving things forward comes out of the replies given to questions raised by the mediator or collaborative practitioners. Being curious also helps creativity, which is essential for the mediation and collaborative processes to work.

3. Create a bridge between the analytical and holistic

This again is one of Nancy Cameron's top tips. As mediators and collaborative practitioners, we have to be analytical but we must also be acutely aware of emotions and feelings. It is important that we know our limits and boundaries and when to bring in other professionals but we are the stepping stone when we bring others in and our clients look to us to know what to do and suggest for the best.

4. Use the Resolution *Parenting after Parting* resources

These resources and particularly the booklet *Divorce and Separation: Choosing the Right Process for You* (Resolution, 2009), and the Resolution website (**www.resolution.org.uk**) provide really good information for parents. Consider using them and providing mediation and collaborative clients with them at first meetings where children are involved. Even if the clients say that there are no real children issues or that the children are fine, the booklets should still be given and the clients should be urged to read them as the information is helpful and could assist at a later date.

5. Seating

Getting the seating right is critical. A round table is much better for mediation and collaborative meetings so that everyone can see each other properly. If you have to use a rectangular or square table, however, make sure the clients are on one side whether you are the mediator or collaborative practitioner as otherwise you can miss some of the all important body language, signs of emotion being displayed.

6. Remain client centred

Remember at all times that this is very much a client-led, client-focused and client-centred process. It is the client who makes the informed decision to undertake the collaborative process and they must feel they are buying in to the process. It is imperative to work carefully at the outset on an anchor statement which keeps the clients anchored to the process when things get stroppy! Forget the anchor statement at your peril!

7. Be organised!

It's critical when dealing with a collaborative case that you stick to the timetable you set, and that you plan and prepare well (as per tip 1). As such, you need to be organised and committed to the process and leave sufficient time to deal with the planning that is required. If you are very busy, perhaps you should consider whether taking on that next new exciting collaborative case is the right thing to do, or whether it would be preferable for the client to be referred to another collaborative colleague – another case will almost certainly wing its way to you in due course.

8. Thorny legal issues

Generally speaking, the minutes of meetings and option development are without prejudice until the final agreement is reached. Financial disclosure is generally open and easily transportable into litigation if the collaborative process breaks down. However, care needs to be taken when analysing the status, e.g. aspirational budgets used with a view to attempting to settle the case – these can be marked 'without prejudice' and attributed that status if agreed.

9. Creative solutions for wide-ranging cases

Remember that collaborative law is not limited just to ancillary relief and Children Act questions. How about using the collaborative law process for prenuptial or post-nuptial agreements, precivil partnerships and cohabitation agreements? It is an ideal forum for dealing with these sorts of issues since the clients at the early stages of their relationship will almost certainly be less positional and antagonistic than when trying to resolve issues arising on separation and divorce.

10. Use all resources you can

There are a number of barristers trained in the collaborative process and they can be used either as joint legal experts, or alternatively for each party as additional members of the team. This is a great new development and we should remember to use it wisely.

APPENDIX 2

Further reading

FAMILY MEDIATION

Haynes, J. (1994) *Alternative Dispute Resolution: The Fundamentals of Family Mediation*, Old Bailey Press.

This is the most recent of John Haynes' books and probably the most useful of them for training. It is based on his training course, adapted for the UK by National Family Mediation of England. It provides a very good overview of Dr Haynes' model of mediation, on which most UK models have drawn.

Mosten, F. S. (1997) *The Complete Guide to Mediation*, American Bar Association.

Another lawyers' book, this is truly a comprehensive guide to all aspects of family mediation for lawyers, including e.g. chapters on 'setting up a mediation-friendly law office', 'lawyer review of the mediated agreement', 'preventing future conflict', 'new mediation-related service products' (including the author's speciality, unbundling) and 'mediation's legacy: the family law system of the future'. This may need to be obtained on the internet through the author's website (**www.mostenmediation.com**).

Parkinson, L. (1997) *Family Mediation*, Sweet & Maxwell.

Lisa Parkinson shares with Resolution many common principles and approaches. Her book is extremely well written and comprehensive and will be of enormous value to Resolution mediators. It provides a useful reminder of the process and skills and contains valuable tips on language and strategies.

COLLABORATIVE LAW

Bishop, G. (2010) *A Client's Guide to Collaborative Divorce – Putting Your Family First,* Family Law in Partnership (**www.flip.co.uk**).

This book is set out in easy to read sections with conversational English. This guide is easy to navigate and explains in detail how the approach works. An invaluable resource for clients.

Isenhart, M. Warren and Spangle, M. (2000) *Collaborative Approaches to Resolving Conflict*, Sage.

This broadens the collaborative approach to look at the best ways to approach conflict and provides a good overview of the overall field of conflict resolution.

Shields, R. W., Ryan, J. P. and Smith, V. L. (2003) *Collaborative Family Law: Another Way to Resolve Family Disputes*, Carswell.

A Canadian textbook offering a guide to the collaborative law process in Canada.

Tesler, P. H. (2008) *Collaborative Law: Achieving Effective Resolution in Divorce without Litigation*, American Bar Association, 2nd edn.

This handbook is a classic from the well-known collaborative law trainer, explaining the emerging dispute resolution model of collaborative practice.

Tesler, P. H. and Thompson, P. (2006) *Collaborative Divorce: The Revolutionary New Way to Restructure Your Family, Resolve Legal Issues and Move on with Your Life*, Regan Books, 2nd edn.

MEDIATION: OTHER RELEVANT READING

Bush, R. B. and Folger, J. (2004) *The Promise of Mediation: The Transformative Approach to Conflict*, Jossey-Bass, rev. edn.

This is the definitive work introducing the author's concept of transformative mediation which has become very popular amongst many US practitioners, though other mediators find the model unhelpful when dealing with parties who expect a resolution of their issues. The model's focus is empowerment and recognition, while settlement is not regarded as a primary concern. The transformation view reflects the capacity of mediation to transform the individuals in dispute and society generally. A practical as well as philosophical consideration of mediation.

Folberg, J. and Milne, A. (eds) (1989) *Divorce Mediation: Theory and Practice*, Guildford Publications.

This hardback book is not a practice manual but rather a collection of chapters by different authors, all experienced practitioners, covering different aspects of divorce mediation. Some chapters are less valuable than others, but overall it provides a clear and valuable insight into the different aspects of divorce mediation theory and practice.

Goodman, A. H. (2004) *Basic Skills for the Mediator*, Solomon, 2nd edn.

From a US perspective, this is a practical basic guide for new mediators with a bias towards commercial mediators.

James, P. (1997) *The Divorce Mediation Handbook: Everything You Need to Know*, Jossey-Bass.

A guide for couples going through mediation.

Monk, G. and Winslade, J. (2000) *Narrative Mediation: A New Approach to Conflict Resolution*, Jossey-Bass.

Narrative mediation starts from the premise that everyone has their own story and each differs. Interesting insights and useful perspectives.

Zaidel, S. R. (1990) *Divorce with Respect: A Guide to Divorce Mediation in Israel*, Haifa.

Israel's divorce laws are different from England's so one would not imagine recommending an Israeli book on mediation for English trainers. However, the general principles that Susan Zaidel outlines, and her simple, commonsense approach make this a readable and useful book.

FAMILIES, MARRIAGE, SEPARATION AND DIVORCE

Ahrons, C. (1995) *The Good Divorce*, Harper Paperbacks.

Divorce can often be a positive thing argues the author, if the translation from marriage to separation can be made while still connecting as parents.

Clout, I. (2005) *The Which Guide to Divorce: The Essential Practical Guide to the Legal and Financial Arrangements for Divorce*, Which? Books, 8th edn.

A practical guide to the legal ins and outs of divorce. How to seek mediation before deciding to split and, if the worst comes, how to smooth matters. This edition by a Resolution trainer includes a mediation section. (A later edition with a new author is now available.)

Gray, J. (1993) *Men are from Mars, Women are from Venus*, Thorsons.

The ideas explored in this book have filtered into our everyday language and the book itself almost seems a little outdated. First published in 1993, *Men are from Mars, Women are from Venus* has become an international publishing phenomenon and is one of the most famous non-fiction publications of all time. Learn what makes members of the opposite sex tick; how to understand their verbal and non-verbal language; how to motivate the opposite sex, avoid arguments and get what you want; how to keep your love alive.

Hetherington, E. M. and Kelly, J. (2002) *For Better or for Worse – Divorce Reconsidered*, W.W. Norton & Co.

A book published in the US, which provides a more reasoned and careful look at the outcomes of divorce in America. This follows up 30 years of research involving 1,400 families of divorce. It provides a more nuanced picture of marital breakup, not as a momentary event, but as a life process that yields continuing influence throughout stages of divorce, single parenthood, remarriage, stepfamily life and other internal personal contexts.

Katzenberg, S. E. (1999) *I Want a Divorce? A Unique Approach to the Emotional and Legal Implications of Marital Crisis*, Kyle Cathie.

This is an excellent guide for clients facing divorce and/or separation and explores the emotional spectrum and the likely stages to be faced by people as they confront the ending of their relationship. Written by a family lawyer.

Maclean, M. (1991) *Surviving Divorce: Women's Resources after Separation*, New York University Press.

An analysis of divorce and its causes and consequences, particularly from the perspective of women and children.

Robinson, M. and Smith, D. (1993) *Step by Step: Focus on Stepfamilies*, Harvester Wheatsheaf.

Issues for stepfamilies arising after the death, separation or divorce of parents. Margaret Robinson is an eminent therapist with the Institute of Family Therapy and has made significant contributions to family law and mediation. Donna Smith is a marital and family therapist. The book covers legal, financial and relationship issues.

Skynner, R. and Cleese, J. (1996) *Families and How to Survive Them*, William Heinemann Ltd.

This must rate as one of the most highly recommended family books available. Its insights are timeless and it has the merit of being written in a delightfully light style, illustrated by genuinely funny cartoons. It is a book that is not only worth reading personally, but also worth recommending to clients.

Troupp, C. (1997) *Couples Counsel*, Cassell Illustrated.

This book deals with understanding problems in relationships. It examines the roles we unconsciously assume when we become part of a couple and the patterns of behaviour inherited from our upbringing. Looks at what happens when a third party upsets the balance, whether it be a new baby or one partner's infidelity. It discusses good communication, why sex and anger are so difficult to deal with, and how partnerships change over time.

Vaughan, D. (1992) *Uncoupling – The Turning Points in Intimate Relationships*, Vintage Books.

This book delineates the underlying pattern beneath every disintegrating relationship and sheds light on a number of key issues, such as why some people never psychologically separate. It explains the dynamics of intimate relationships, married or not, straight or gay and the way in which people separate from them.

Wallerstein, J. and Blakeslee, S. (1996) *The Good Marriage: How and Why Love Lasts*, Grand Central Publishing.

Critically acclaimed, this book seemed initially destined for success but has not had the powerful impact of *Surviving the Break-up*. This book is an examination of how and why good marriages work. Very readable and interesting.

Reibstein, J. and Bamber, R. (1997) *The Family through Divorce: How You Can Limit the Damage*, Thorsons.

This book offers expert advice on how to manage all of the legal and emotional aspects of divorce, written by a leading collaborative lawyer (Roger Bamber) and psychiatrist (Janet Reibstein).

CONFLICT MANAGEMENT THEORY AND NEGOTIATION

Acland, A. F. (1995) *Resolving Disputes Without Going to Court: A Consumer Guide to Alternative Dispute Resolution*, Century, 2nd edn.

This is specifically aimed at the consumers of dispute resolution services, primarily in the commercial sphere, rather than practitioners. It is easily readable, written in short chapters.

Bevan, A. (1992) *Alternative Dispute Resolution*, Waterlow.

Also personal and anecdotal in style, this is a foundation book in ADR, concentrating on mediation.

Brown, H. and Marriott, A. (1999) *ADR Principles and Practice*, Sweet & Maxwell, 2nd edn.

This is an author's review! A comprehensive work of over 650 pages examining all aspects of ADR with a particular focus on different models of mediation in all fields of activity. Gives attention to the evaluation processes, with an extended section on family issues; also covers ethics, confidentiality, drafting and many other aspects of dispute resolution practice. It is geared primarily for those who have or intend to develop dispute resolution practices.

Crawley, J. (1995) *Constructive Conflict Management: Managing to Make a Difference*, Nicolas Brealey Publishing.

One of the foremost books on conflict resolution, this contains explanations and self-help exercises, including a section on mediation. Covers a range of kinds of conflicts including those that occur in the workplace.

De Bono, E. (1991) *Conflicts: A Better Way to Resolve Them*, Penguin Books.

Edward De Bono is one of the best-known lateral thinkers of modern times and looks at map making of a conflict and then using lateral thinking to generate alternative solutions.

Dickson, A. (2006) *Difficult Conversations: What to Say in Tricky Situations without Ruining the Relationship*, Piatkus Books.

We all find ourselves in difficult situations where we need to tread lightly – or deal with the consequences. But how often do we say nothing – or say too much? This book aims to help the reader to step back from their own emotions, remain calm and work out the right thing to say. It has practical advice and examples ranging from difficult discussions with your partner, friends and family, to salespeople, bosses and colleagues, showing first the wrong way – and then the right way – to get through those tricky times.

Doyle, M. (2000) *Advising on ADR: The Essential Guide to Appropriate Dispute Resolution*, Advice Services Alliance.

An outline of dispute resolution processes in the UK to facilitate broad understanding and referrals. A very useful and recommended handbook.

Fisher, R., Ury, W. and Patton, B. (2003) *Getting to Yes: Negotiating an Agreement without Giving in*, Random House Business Books, 2nd edn.

This seminal book uncovers the secrets to successful negotiation. Nowadays, hardly anyone gets through the day without a single negotiation, yet, few of us are armed with the effective, powerful negotiating skills that prevent stubborn haggling and ensure mutual problem solving. Fisher and Ury cut through the jargon to present a few easily remembered principles that will guide you, no matter what the other side does. They include: don't bargain over positions; separate people from the problem; insist on objective criteria. And what if they won't play?

Harper, G. (2004) *The Joy of Conflict Resolution: Transforming Victims, Villains and Heroes in the Workplace and at Home*, New Society Publishers.

Gerald Monk, author of *Narrative Mediation*, comments that 'this is a valuable read for anyone wanting a quick and accessible understanding of the conflict that has captured them and how to get out of it'.

McConnon, S. and McConnon, M. (2004) *Resolving Conflict: How to Manage Disagreements and Develop Trust and Understanding*, How To Books Ltd, 2nd edn.

More of a workplace-oriented book. This nonetheless gives a fairly simple guide to understand and resolve conflictual problems.

Macfarlane, J. (ed.) (1997) *Rethinking Disputes: The Mediation Alternative*, Routledge Cavendish.

A compilation of contributions by different authors on the use of mediation and ADR in different fields within the UK, Canada and Australia.

Patterson, K., Grenny, J., McMillan, R. and Switzler, A. (2004) *Crucial Conversations: Tools for Talking about Violated Expectations and Broken Promises*, McGraw-Hill Professional.

Crucial conversations are interpersonal exchanges at work or at home that we dread having but know we cannot avoid. How do you say what needs to be said while avoiding an argument with a boss, child, or relationship partner? *Crucial Conversations* offers readers a proven seven-point strategy for achieving their goals in all those emotionally, psychologically, or legally charged situations that can arise in their professional and personal lives. Based on the authors' DialogueSmart training seminars, the techniques are geared toward getting people to lower their defences, creating mutual respect and understanding, increasing emotional safety, and encouraging freedom of expression.

Rosenberg, M. B. (2003) *Non-violent Communication: A Language of Life*, Puddledancer Press US, 2nd edn.

An enlightening look at how peaceful communication can create compassionate connections with family, friends, and other acquaintances. The book uses stories, examples, and sample dialogues to provide solutions to communication problems both at home and in the workplace. Non-violent communication skills are fully explained and can be applied to personal, professional, and political differences. Included in this new edition is information on how to compassionately connect with oneself.

Stone, D., Patton, B. and Heen, S. with foreword by Fisher, R. (2000) *Difficult Conversations: How to Discuss What Matters Most*, Penguin Books.

Asking for a rise, ending a relationship, saying no to someone in need. At work, home, and across the garden fence, difficult conversations are attempted or avoided every day. This book aims to show the reader how to manage their emotions and deal with these difficult conversations.

This book has spawned a series of 'difficult conversations' books, including *Difficult Conversations: What to Say in Tricky Situations Without Ruining the Relationship*, and *Crucial Conversations: Tools for Talking about Violated Expectations and Broken Promises*.

Ury, W. (1992) *Getting Past No: Negotiating with Difficult People*, Random House Business Books.

This book provides a step-by-step method for negotiation that aims to ensure that satisfactory agreement is reached with even the most intransigent people. The author also co-wrote *Getting Past Yes*. He tackles the area in which the original work suffered adverse comment and subtitles this work *Negotiating with Difficult People*. This book covers some of the missing ground, but there are those who still feel that there may be other ways also of having to deal with difficult negotiators.

EMOTIONS AND COMMUNICATION SKILLS

Bolton, R. (1986) *How to Assert Yourself, Listen to Others and Resolve Conflicts*, Touchstone.

A communication skills handbook to help eliminate communication problems.

Folger, J. and Jones, T. S. (eds) (1994) *New Directions in Mediation: Communication Research and Perspectives*, Sage.

This paperback comprises a series of chapters by contributors who all review mediation from a communications perspective. Primarily a theoretical work, written mainly by university academics, and sometimes using specialist communications language, it also has a section by practitioners dedicated to translating these ideas into practice.

Goleman, D. P. (2005) *Emotional Intelligence*, Bantam Books.

A seminal work which redefined intelligence and success to include emotional intelligence and describes in some detail how our emotions play a far greater role in thought, decision making and individual success than is commonly acknowledged. A very important book for lawyers to read.

Hammond, C. (2005) *Emotional Rollercoaster*, Fourth Estate.

This book explores the mushrooming research on emotions, to question how the brain and body interact to produce emotions and what, if anything, we can do to harness them.

McFarlan, B. (2005) *Drop the Pink Elephant: 15 Ways to Say What You Mean . . . and Mean What You Say*, Capstone Publishing Ltd.

In a fun book on communication skills, *Drop the Pink Elephant*, Bill McFarlan reveals how to avoid the deadly trap of allowing poor communication patterns to obscure your meaning and reduce your effectiveness. *Drop the Pink Elephant* is filled with helpful, simple and practical advice on how to make your words count for more.

Pease, A. (1981) *Body Language*, Sheldon Press.

A useful book to provide an introduction to the subject. Its value lies in the awareness it engenders in relation to non-verbal communications, rather than its examples necessarily being definitive as ways to read the body.

Pease, A. and Pease, B. (1999) *Why Men Don't Listen and Women Can't Read Maps*, Pease Training.

Left-brain and right-brain distinctions indicate whether a person will respond with a dominance towards logic and rationality or intuition. The authors extend this to argue for an evolutionary distinction between the way in which men's and women's brains function. Would support the general world view expressed by John Gray. A valuable insight into brain functioning, whether or not the underlying gender premise is accepted.

CHILDREN

Books for adults (professionals and parents)

Cockett, M. and Tripp, J. (1994) *Exeter Family Study, Family Breakdown and its Impact on Children*, University of Exeter Press.

This study of intact and re-ordered families is important reading, extending UK research on children to complement work done in the US.

De'Ath, E. (1988) *Step-Parenting*, Family Doctor Publications.

A short booklet (48 pages) outlining difficulties of step-parenting and offering information and advice.

Goldstein, S. (1987) *Divorced Parenting: How to Make It Work*, Methuen.

Mitchell, A. K. (1985) *Children in the Middle: Living through Divorce*, Tavistock.

Schaffer, H. R. (1998) *Making Decisions about Children: Psychological Questions and Answers*, WileyBlackwell, 2nd edn.

This research-based book covers practical matters. It is described as bridging the gap with academia. Aimed at professionals working with children, it deals with issues that family lawyers and mediators are bound to face.

Wallerstein, J. and Kelly, J. (1989) *Surviving the Break-Up*, Grant McIntyre (out of print).

Wells, R. (2003) *Helping Children to Cope with Divorce: Overcoming Common Problems*, Sheldon Press, 3rd edn.

Books written for children

Many authors of books for children and young adults have written books focusing on fictional stories where the characters have to deal with separation and divorce within their families. The titles listed below are a very small sample:

Bryant-Mole, K. (1996) *What's Happening? Splitting Up*, Wayland Books.

One of a series for children at school and with their families. This one looks at divorce.

Harding, C. and Eccles, J. (1994) *Stepping out: Can Brook Survive her Stepfamily?*, Macmillan Children's Books.

For children over 11 years old, this is a teenager's letters to a friend.

Kransy Brown, L. and Brown, M. (1993) *Dinosaur's Divorce: A Guide for Changing Families*, Little, Brown & Co.

A cartoon strip story explaining separation, divorce and reparenting for very young children from ages 3 to 5 upwards. Generally a very well regarded book.

Other tools

The Victoria Chart Company produce the *My Time* chart designed for children aged 4 to 10 years. This is a time planner for two-home families with young children. It lets children know when they are spending time with each parent. Details can be obtained from Victoria Time Charts (**www.encourageandpraise.com**) or from the Resolution website (**www.resolution.org.uk**)

APPENDIX 3

Resolution website resources

Up-to-date versions of the following are available on the Resolution website for members:

- Precedent agreement to mediate
- Guidelines for mediators working in court
- Privilege in the ADR context
- Precedent participation agreement (PA) – no children
- Precedent PA – Children
- Precedent PA – Pre-marriage and civil partnership agreement – no children
- Precedent PA – Pre-marriage and civil partnership agreement – children
- Precedent PA – Cohabitation – no children
- Precedent PA – Cohabitation – children
- Precedent PA for financial consultant
- Terms of business – a sample letter for collaborative practitioners
- Collaborative process principles
- Ethical standards
- Collaborative practice protocol
- Process map diagram
- Paper on Proceeds of Crime Act
- Client preparation sheet
- Giving advice in the collaborative process
- POD guidelines
- Collaborative research
- Privilege following the breakdown of the collaborative process – a guide for professionals
- The role of the family consultant
- Collaborative research form
- Resolution ADR section membership rules

APPENDIX 4

The settlement team

Stu Webb, JD

[This article was first published by IACP in the *Collaborative Review*, Volume 10, Issue 3: Winter 2009.]

Most of us know by now that we have only one collaborative rule – the disclaimer clause: the agreement to withdraw from the case if settlement is not reached. It is also the rule that some professionals have difficulty with. You might hear them say, 'Why have this rule? I try to settle all of my cases.' Or, 'I couldn't possibly abandon my client!'

Most of us who practice collaboratively know instinctively why we have the rule, but let's run down some of the reasons:

- Without the rule, our settlement process would be colored by, and anticipate the possibility of, going to trial. The attorneys are forced to be the part-time warrior (litigator) and the part-time peacemaker (collaborator) at the same time, bringing his or her full attention to neither role.
- Fear drives the litigation process and interferes with the settlement process. If the clients are not sure that they are protected from litigation, they have a hard time letting go of their fear.
- Without the rule, we would be careful how we communicate with the other client and the client's attorney for fear that we might be perceived as not zealously advocating for our client.
- Without the rule, we might be tempted to use one-sided experts rather than using neutral experts to bolster our position at trial.
- The rule allows the clients and the collaborative team all to be aligned. Everyone's interest is to find the settlement structure that satisfies as many of the clients' interests as possible.
- The rule allows us to work with our clients in a positive, open settlement climate where the clients feel safe to express their needs and interests without the fear that someone in the room might someday be cross-examining them.
- Without the rule, the settlement professionals would be locked into preparing for and participating in litigation – a process that would take financial and emotional resources away from helping clients resolve their cases.
- Settlements in the litigation process have a tone that separates the parties through adversarial practices. Settlements reached on the courthouse steps often lack the creativity that can be generated by a settlement team using the structured collaborative process.
- Clients feel the need to protect themselves when they feel threatened, as they do in litigation. Clients are afraid to be generous and thoughtful when they feel they are being attacked.
- When a collaborative case doesn't completely settle, the clients will have the best of two approaches: work with a settlement team and work with litigation experts.

- Collaborative practitioners, freed by the rule, are trained in settlement modes and frames of reference to enhance the possibilities that the clients will be able to achieve settlement in the collaborative process.

Having participated in hundreds of collaborative cases, I'll speak briefly about my experience as a litigating lawyer, my experience as a collaborative lawyer and team member, and the impact of the rule requiring withdrawal in collaborative cases.

As a litigating lawyer, I merged with my client and his or her positions. I was a spokesperson for those issues and the stage manager for presenting them to the opposing counsel and the court. I was invested with my client's case and felt personally gratified when the client 'won' and devastated when the client 'lost' the case. My task was one of performance, and I felt the personal pressures that come with performance expectations. My relationship with the opposing counsel was cool and my relationship with the other spouse was practically nonexistent. Settlement talks, when they existed, were conducted by the attorneys, were argument-based and usually conducted outside the presence of the clients (unless in mandated settlement conferences).

So isn't it dramatic, the difference the rule makes in the collaborative process? That simple rule converts the litigating lawyer into a settlement lawyer (assuming the lawyer has made the requisite paradigm shift). As a collaborative lawyer, I am no longer involved with orchestrating how to achieve what I perceive as my client's position. I am involved with providing support for my client and the entire settlement space. I want to ensure that the clients are participating fully in the process. It's their process. I help them decide what kind of a team they want to assist them in the settlement process. I let go of the outcome, after providing requested legal input. I feel collegial toward the other spouse's lawyer and warmly toward the other spouse. I am concerned about the welfare of the parties' children. I encourage the parties to enunciate their goals and shape their results in a way that is consistent with their interests.

While the above are some of the functions of collaboration, the hardest aspect to articulate is the tremendous feeling of well-being I experience when I do this work, knowing that I, together with the other members of the settlement team, am assisting a family in reshaping their relationship often in positive ways.

APPENDIX 5

Visions of excellence

Henry Brown

[A talk given to the Resolution Alternative Dispute Resolution conference in Bath, 16 September 2006.]

As professionals, we all aspire to achieve excellence in our work, but I'm not sure that 'excellence' has a clear meaning in the context of marriage breakdown and family work and that's what I'd like to examine today.

I'm not interested in the dictionary definition, but rather the concept. I find that words with important meanings can get devalued. For example, a friend of mine who is an academic said to me, 'Whenever I hear someone use the phrase "quality assured" I think, oh oh – another funding cut.'

I'd like to consider some random and totally arbitrary aspects of excellence. I'll do so in six propositions specifically in relation to marriage breakdown and family law and practice. My first proposition is:

Proposition No. 1: Family practitioners are, by and large, not brain surgeons

I practised as a commercial mediator as well as a family mediator and am very interested in the concept of risk analysis in the commercial field. I've been involved in devising a risk analysis questionnaire that helps parties to assess their level of risk in litigating, not just on the basis of the legal risk, but having regard to all the wider issues that apply to each side.

This questionnaire raises a number of questions for parties to consider, and I sometimes hand it to parties to complete for their own purposes, and not to hand back to me. It struck me as I was preparing this talk that something similar could be a valuable tool in family work.

Anyway, in one of the talks I went to about risk analysis, the speaker made a point that we needed as lawyers to be more analytical about the risks of litigating and that it was not good enough simply to say to clients, 'I think you have about a 60% prospect of success,' without any proper analysis or detail.

The speaker made the further point that if someone went to a brain surgeon to consider the possibility of brain surgery, they would not be satisfied with the surgeon saying, 'My instinct tells me that you have about a 60% prospect of survival.'. They would want to have scans taken and detailed explanations of what was involved. They would want to know how to improve their prospects of survival, and what alternative options there were to surgery, and to have proper analyses of those alternatives.

I agree with the speaker on most of what he said, but there is a big difference between brain surgery and family law. Apart from the difference in the life-threatening implications of brain surgery, it seems to me that another main difference lies in the fact that there is a much greater element of objectivity in assessing brain function and malfunction than there is in assessing family breakdown and outcomes.

Family work is so complex and has so many uncertainties and imponderables that objective analyses are very hard to make. By the same token, assessing excellence in the context of family work is similarly difficult to objectify in advance. We can look at something that was done and consider whether or not it was excellent, but it's much harder to lay down hard and fast rules as to what constitutes excellence in specific cases when looking ahead generally.

I think of Lord Justice Scrutton's reference to the definition of an elephant, namely, 'I may not be able to define an elephant, but I know one when I see it.' Excellence is rather like that. We may not be able to define it with precision, but we know it when we see it. But as we see through different eyes and different perspectives, what may seem excellent to one person may be viewed as poor by another. And we don't have scans or objective criteria to help us identify excellence in specific cases.

Some aspects of excellence can be objectively assessed. The Law Society for example has a *Client Care/Practice Excellence* training package for practice management and a quality mark *Lexcel* which aims at, 'standards of excellence in areas such as client care, case management and risk management'. My experience is that the mark can assess the objective elements, but doesn't purport to address the quality of lawyering. Which is understandable because here you're entering into a more complex and subjective area.

It's rather like having a dictionary definition of excellence that can tell you what it is, but doesn't tell you how it applies in specific instances.

How does one identify excellence when one enters the fraught area of marriage breakdown, with its range of potential issues concerning status, children, property, finance, living standards and future security and the complexities of adults' and children's needs, both material and emotional? Not only does every situation have its own circumstances and needs, but every client brings his or her own world view.

I remember sitting on a bus some years ago and overhearing a snatch of a conversation between a rather exasperated mother and her eight or nine year old son. The mother said to him, 'Why must you always argue about everything?' to which he replied, 'I'm not arguing, I'm only telling the truth.' That exchange profoundly encapsulates many of the issues faced by family practitioners, whether lawyers, counsellors, mediators or judges. That deep, absolute belief in one's own truth, whether expressed in the law office, the mediation room, the court or dressed as Batman at the top of Tower Bridge.

What a challenge for family practitioners! As professionals in this field, we can offer help, guidance, advice and support, which will vary according to the needs of each client and family. We do the best for the client and the family that is possible and appropriate in their particular circumstances.

But who is to judge whether this constitutes excellence? The client? Or the client's partner, who may have quite a contrary view? Or the children of the family, if they could be consulted about what they thought about the way their parents and the lawyers handled the situation? Or the media, who would probably judge the merits of the lawyers based on the level of capital settlement? Or the lawyers themselves? Or their peers, other lawyers and family professionals who from a distance might wonder whether there might have been a better way to resolve the case?

This is not an argument for abandoning an aspiration to excellence, or for throwing up one's hands and saying that there can't be any criteria, but rather a recognition that excellence may mean no more than making the best of very difficult and challenging circumstances, and that it comes in many different shapes and forms. Which takes us to . . .

Proposition No. 2: Excellence does not preclude paradox, uncertainty or imperfection

This proposition is about not putting excellence into some kind of ivory tower, when it's often a product of moving through uncertain and murky territory, going for the best you can even when you know that it's not absolutely right, or that, like Alice through the Looking Glass, you may have to go in the opposite direction to find what you're looking for.

Isn't it paradoxical that one of the most significant breakthroughs in the Middle East in the last few decades arose in the 1978 Camp David talks, mediated by President Jimmy Carter, and involving not two peace-loving liberal leaders, but the right-wing Prime Minister of Israel, Menachim Begin, and President Sadat of Egypt, who had led Egypt into the 1973 Yom Kippur war against Israel?

Some of you will know my friend and colleague, Robert Benjamin, an American mediator who has done training work for Resolution. He writes extensively about the frailties, oddities, and paradoxes inherent in working as a mediator in the family field.

Robert refers to the paradox in negotiation that arises in that negotiators need to be authentic but sometimes also have to appear to be authentic when they are not. Consequently, he says, authenticity, while anchored in genuine integrity, might at times be part ruse.

This fits in with what Lax and Sebenius say in their book, *The Manager as Negotiator*. They believe that even when people adopt a cooperative problem-solving approach, they may well still aim to achieve the best outcome for themselves within this different mode of negotiating, and that there is what they call an *essential tension* between competitive and problem-solving approaches.

Far from ivory towering mediation, Robert Benjamin takes a tongue-in-cheek downbeat view of the skills of mediation. I know of nobody more committed to excellence than Robert, but he resists becoming overawed by the seriousness of the process.

Robert has distilled four attributes of the natural mediator: confused, voyeuristic, compulsive and marginal.

Confusion, he says, allows a mediator to understand that there are no easy answers, that heroes can be scoundrels, and victims can be perpetrators, and vice versa; that it's never easy or clear.

The second he says is voyeurism which he defines not in a sexual context but as an endless fascination with how human beings engage with each other, construct their realities, and pursue their intimate relations. This attribute allows the mediator a greater ability to resist being judgmental, knowing that 'there but for the grace of God, go I.'

The third attribute of the natural mediator he says is compulsiveness, and obsessively working at the details in order to bring order out of chaos.

The fourth he reckons is to be marginal, on the fringe – an outsider – less concerned about what is right, than with what will work to settle a dispute in the present circumstance. It means, he says, 'letting go of attachments to what life should be in a perfect world'.

And on this subject, I want to quote another American mediator, Lenard Marlow who has the following definition of mediation. He says, 'Mediation is an imperfect procedure that employs an imperfect third person to help two imperfect people reach an imperfect agreement in an imperfect world.'

Robert Benjamin has also written about having to work with flawed understandings. So it is no surprise to find that in his writings, Robert Benjamin describes Lenard Marlow's definition as apt.

I regard these thoughts from Lenard Marlow and Robert Benjamin as having a meaningful underlying message, even though written in fun. I reckon that Marlow's notion of imperfection accurately describes the conditions that we commonly work under and from which we have to help create the best outcome available, whatever process we use. Excellence is carved out of this very hard stone.

The critical point seems to me to be that whether we're working in mediation, collaborative family law practice or in the traditional way, excellence doesn't lie in some pure and idealised form but rather in helping to create something reasonable if imperfect out of something that may be unclear, paradoxical, imperfect and very often messy.

I'm reminded of the story of the rabbi in old Eastern Europe long ago, who was walking through the village when he came across two people engaged in a dispute. They asked the rabbi to express his view and one of the disputants then proceeded to tell his side of the story. When the rabbi had heard the first party he told him, 'You're absolutely right.' The other party was upset and said, 'Rabbi, that's not fair, you haven't yet heard my side of the story.' 'Oh, I'm so sorry,' said the rabbi, 'please do tell me'. When the other party had told his story, the rabbi said, 'You're absolutely right.' A bystander remonstrated with the rabbi, saying, 'Rabbi, you've told the one person he's absolutely right and you've told the other person that he's absolutely right. They can't both be absolutely right.' The rabbi turned to the bystander and said, 'You know, you're absolutely right.'

Proposition No. 3: Rigidified excellence is a contradiction in terms

Understandably, we have a tendency to regulate processes in order to ensure some form of quality control. That's of course inherent in professional qualification and practice of all kinds. I've been involved in it myself, in specifying practice and accreditation criteria for the FMA, for Resolution mediators, for the UK College of Family Mediators and for the Law Society's mediation panels and for its accredited mediation training bodies.

Although I was part of this regulatory process, I'm concerned that family mediation may have become over-regulated. Family lawyer mediators, for example, have to undergo training, aim for accreditation with their mediation organisations, have professional practice consultancy and CPD, and may also have to conform to the requirements of the Law Society and the UK College of Family Mediators. On top of all that, if they want to do publicly funded work, which is where by far the greatest volume of family mediation lies, they will also have to have a Legal Services Commission franchise or contract and comply with the LSC's requirements as to their Quality Mark standard for family mediation.

Of course, I understand why practice regulations are needed. Government and the courts want to be sure that mediators, especially if they're publicly funded, are properly qualified. But once mediators are properly trained and judged as competent, I wonder whether there really is a need for such stringent controls. Once solicitors are qualified as such, they are left to get on with it, subject obviously to ethical constraints and CPD requirements.

In the commercial mediation field, there isn't any regulation and I'm not aware of any problems arising from unregulated practice. A new umbrella body, the Civil Mediation Council, is proposing a minimal form of control for limited purposes, for example for the National Mediation Helpline, by accrediting providers and requiring mediators to belong to an accredited provider. Accreditation is a relatively simple exercise for providers. This indicates the relatively minimalist approach that can be taken to regulation.

But accepting the need for some form of regulation, I would nevertheless argue against rigidifying any processes, whether in mediation or collaborative law, and whether by way of Code, regulation or just the way it is thought about. By rigidifying process, I am referring to attempts to fix procedures as articles of faith which are actually just preferred procedures.

To take just one example, the UK College Code on family mediation stipulates that a mediator will not maintain separate confidences as between the parties. This is absolute, and there is no provision to allow them to agree otherwise. Similarly it provides that a mediator can't say anything to one lawyer that will not also be said to the other.

That is based on one model of practice and doesn't allow for the fact that the mediator and the couple may agree to use a different model, namely one in which the mediator may shuttle between the parties to try to work out terms, maintaining separate confidences between them. This is the standard model used in civil and commercial disputes, and one that I have also used effectively in family issues.

I think for example of a very high conflict divorce that I mediated, in which every possible issue was contentious. The couple were able to talk to one another and we had lots of sessions, but they always seemed to go round in circles. Every time we appeared to make progress, something would happen between sessions, and either the police would be called in, or the social services, or some financial crisis would arise. And because there was a substantial family trust involved, financial discussions were laborious and depended on one of the parties reverting to the trustees.

Eventually I set up a commercial-type session with them and their lawyers for most of a day, which the Chairman of the trustees attended for a time. We had joint and separate meetings, and during the separate meetings, with each party and their lawyer in a separate room, I shuttled for much of the day, maintaining separate confidences in each room, except as I was authorised to release, subject only to the condition that any financial disclosure in the separate meeting would be open. This flouted all received wisdom about people not being able to stay in the process for more than 1½ hours or so, about not maintaining separate confidences, and about the perceived disadvantages of having lawyers directly involved in the process. The couple coped very well with an all-day session, the separate confidences helped to cut through enormously, and both parties' lawyers were consistently helpful.

In the event, that meeting was a major contribution to the settlement that eventually followed, covering the divorce itself, which had been defended, all financial issues and the creation of an agreed parenting plan.

I can see no good reason for rigidifying the rules disallowing this, and every reason to allow parties freedom to agree other procedures. And using this model – or any other – there seems no reason to insist that the mediator can't have separate and independent communications with the respective lawyers.

I mention this as an example of the ways in which we box ourselves into corners and set up constraints that go beyond the needs of practice. Because we tended to think about our model in the narrow way that I've mentioned, mediators have generally resisted using this kind of practice and trainers have resisted teaching it.

I think that there is now a greater readiness among mediators to explore different ways of working, and of adapting processes and models.

Many people feel that arbitration lost its way as a process when it abandoned much of its informality and started rigidifying and mimicking the litigation process. That's been redressed in recent years, but we need to avoid that rigidification happening with mediation or collaborative practice.

But whatever the merits may or may not be of having stringent controls over the practice of family mediation or collaborative law, there are very different criteria when one moves beyond establishing competence into the area of providing excellence. Here, I believe that you can provide guidelines, but you can't be prescriptive. Excellence in a straightjacket is a fundamental misconception.

And on the subject of straightjackets, I really wonder why we straightjacket ourselves by so commonly using the phrase 'best practice'? My concern arises from its categorical statement that the practice it outlines purports to be objectively best, and that nothing else is or can be as good or better. Anyone who doesn't follow 'best practice' is at risk of criticism (and perhaps of a negligence claim) when trying to innovate. But I think that the concept of best practice is a near-sighted view that doesn't allow for the likelihood that sooner or later some other practice will almost certainly develop that is as good or better. Best practice inhibits innovation and creativity, without which neither mediation nor collaborative law would exist.

I don't understand what is wrong with referring to good practice? Or if one needs to move to the superlative, then could we not refer to current best or best available practice?

Proposition No. 4: Excellence in family work is arid without humanity

On a couple of occasions, I've gone into legal bookshops and asked if they had books on law and humanity. Each time they've referred me to the section on human rights; but I couldn't find anything on law and humanity. A great deal has been written about human rights law, and about crimes against humanity. What I am interested in is the more mundane question of how lawyers express their common humanity in the everyday practice of law.

Now I know a little – very little indeed – about groups of people, mainly in the United States, who are looking for something more profound in the way they practise law. I have for example read about the Project on Integrating Spirituality, Law and Politics, which aims for a more humane and compassionate view of legal practice.

And I've looked at the website of the Renaissance Lawyer Society, which has a humanistic approach to the law and a vision of 'a legal system based on problem-solving, healing conflicts, and supporting us all in working and living together in peace'. They in turn are looking at ways of working in the law that are compatible with these principles, for example through collaborative law, mediation, restorative justice and community lawyering. These and others like them are interesting developments, albeit involving a tiny minority of lawyers.

I know why I wanted to be a lawyer, originally in South Africa some 50 years ago. It was a respected profession, and one in which I could make a reasonable living; but my main motivation was that I wanted to do something worthwhile. I wanted to be a part of creating a better society, in which law served everyone.

I have no doubt that everyone here today was motivated to some greater or lesser extent in choosing to work in the family field by some sense of wanting to do something worthwhile.

And that is the aspiration and attraction of family ADR: to find a better way of working with people in family crisis, a way that reduces rather than exacerbates their conflict, a way that allows them to move towards some future healing.

In fact, I'd like the sub-title of this talk to be, 'Law, healing and humanity', a combination of concepts that has been in my mind for some time. On a few occasions that I've mentioned this title to others, there has been some surprise at the juxtaposition of these three words, which people don't necessarily associate with one another. 'Why not?' is the question I ask. Can law be a healing profession? What is the relationship between law and common humanity?

These aren't just rhetorical questions, but I think they need to be addressed. There aren't easy answers, because of the infinite variety of ways that law can be practised, that humanity can be expressed and that healing can take place. Clearly, part of the answer lies in why we're here today: the recognition that in addition to their pragmatic value, mediation and collaborative family law are both vehicles that allow for humanity and healing.

What a shame that the legal profession is not perceived as having a capacity for humanity and healing. I understand of course that it has many faces, and that representing people in contentious situations is a major part of what it holds itself out as doing well. I don't see that this needs to change. What perhaps needs to be reviewed is its ability to do whichever is needed of it: knight in shining armour or healer.

I should say that it's not just in ADR or family work that humanity can be expressed as part of the practice of law. I worked as a commercial litigator for over 25 years, and as a commercial mediator for nearly 20 years, and I believe from my personal experience that there is scope in both those fields for lawyers to practise with humanity and compassion. Of course, that often isn't what clients want, and one wouldn't push it onto them, any more than one would push one's own priorities onto family clients. Rather, it is a frame of mind that allows for the possibility of a less hostile way of resolving the issues. In the same way that family lawyers have developed a more civilised approach to family issues, so litigation or commercial lawyers can adapt the way they work, think and communicate.

The way that we think does inevitably influence the way that we work. I remember coming back in 1989 from a conference of the US Academy of Family Mediators in Colorado, where I had spent one of my days there with a conflict resolver called Tom Crum, who not only practised in the field of inter-personal conflict, but also worked as an Aikido instructor. Tom Crum showed us how to bring practice of Aikido into conflict resolution practice, moving responsively with the flow of an attack to unsettle the attacker.

I wasn't convinced about the relevance of this to the real world until I got back to London and received a hostile letter from my opposite number in a divorce case where I was acting for one of the parties. It was a case in which any allegation by one of the couple was immediately countered by a counter allegation against the other. This had been going on for months. Anyway, I didn't respond to the new allegation by taking instructions and counter-attacking as we had been doing. Instead, fortified by Tom Crum and Aikido, I phoned my opposite number and said: 'I have your letter and will take instructions, but if what you say is right then I will ask my client to remedy the position right away. I agree that my client's actions in that situation would be unacceptable.' My opposite number's silent amazement was audible. His whole tone changed and he said he appreciated it. I added that by the same token I'd be grateful if he would check some other allegation my client had made. In his subdued tone, he agreed to do so.

I could hardly believe it, but that marked the change to the whole case, and we were able to move into constructive negotiations and subsequently settle. As a bonus, my client, who had been taking a hard line up to then, softened and many years later told me that the process of resolving the issues as we had done had changed her life.

In my experience, healing isn't about people instantly embracing one another. Rather, it's about working in a way that allows people to do that in their own time and their own way. I'd like to mention by way of example a commercial dispute that I mediated. An elderly father and middle-aged son were involved in a High Court dispute with one another involving the rights in the father's shares in the family business. They hadn't spoken for two or three years. In the mediation, the father's lawyer mentioned in passing that the son was running the business reasonably well. In a private caucusing session with the son, I drew attention to this, and the son said, 'Yes, I was pleased he said that. Actually I learned a lot about the business from my father'. I asked him if he minded if I told his father this, and he agreed. During my following private session with the father, I discussed practical matters and also mentioned what the son had said, to which the father responded, 'Did he say that? He's a good boy really'. He in turn allowed me to carry this sentiment back.

Well, after a day's intense negotiations, involving joint and separate meetings, the matter settled. After they had signed the settlement agreement in a joint meeting and were about to leave, the son leaned over to the father and said, 'I'm glad we've settled.' The father raised his thumb in warm agreement. They then left separately.

I suppose that I had rather hoped to see them physically embrace and walk out together, but on reflection, that was about me and not about them. What we had done was to resolve the dispute at a practical level, end the hostility and leave the space for healing to follow. That's a pattern I've seen many times, and not just in matters involving families.

Although I've talked about healing and humanity, it's not enough to have these as aspirational concepts without the practical means for them to manifest themselves.

If excellence is arid without humanity, then we should also say that humanity and healing are inadequate without effective processes and skilled and knowledgeable application. What we need is to be able to combine our belief in a better way with the actual mechanics and skills of providing it. This may be another paradox, but we need to be hard-headed and pragmatic, highly skilled and very effective if we want our compassion and our humanity to have a practical and tangible outcome.

That's why we need the reliable frameworks that both collaborative practice and mediation provide, and the specialist skills and understandings that we need to learn in order to become excellent collaborative practitioners or mediators.

Which leads me to the fifth proposition . . .

Proposition No. 5: Pure law is not enough

When I trained as a family mediator 21 years ago, conciliation, as it was then called, was a process only used by therapists, counsellors, social workers and other non-lawyer professionals in relation to children's issues. Financial issues were dealt with by the lawyers outside the conciliation process. I joined with Lisa Parkinson, Felicity White, John Cornwell, Jack Bleiman and Diana Parker to run an inter-disciplinary mediation pilot scheme for some 3 years. In it, a lawyer co-mediated with a non-lawyer, and we addressed all the issues arising on separation and divorce. The pilot scheme turned into the Family Mediators' Association.

In the course of developing training for the FMA, we worked extensively with an inter-disciplinary model. For us lawyers, it was an invaluable experience in seeing how different disciplines addressed the same issues, and I believe that the benefits were reciprocal. Even though the FMA no longer exclusively works in the co-mediation model, though it remains its primary model, and even though we developed a sole mediation model in Resolution, the benefits of inter-disciplinary co-operation have very much remained with us.

In creating Resolution's mediation training, we drew not only on our mediation and legal backgrounds, but also on other disciplines to understand and work with couples' issues and dynamics. We appreciated the importance of addressing emotions, and understanding how different people might express their emotions differently. We had regard to systemic thinking, and to patterns of behaviour, looking both at each individual and the family as a whole.

Counsellors and therapists supported the training and brought a richness to it. They did sessions on family systems and dynamics. Children's issues were considered from different perspectives from those that lawyers and judges tended to do. Many of us developed a better understanding of the counselling process and the way in which inter-disciplinary networking could be better achieved and promoted.

I would say that much of the excellence of the mediation process arises from the fact that it has developed from different professional backgrounds; and collaborative practice of course similarly draws on a much wider base than purely legal principles. Involving the clients directly in an interest-based negotiation process, collaborative practice demands sensitive and skilled representation with a family focus and a premium on reasonable cooperation.

In collaborative practice, the availability of a family consultant with a counselling or therapeutic background, working alongside the collaborative lawyer, is an inspired idea that should help to provide each party with practical and emotional support, and enable each to address and hopefully overcome obstacles to progress.

It replicates the principle of inter-disciplinary co-mediation, but with a different dynamic that allows each person the benefit of an individual lawyer and counsellor.

In Resolution's mediation model, counselling or psychotherapy may precede or run parallel with mediation, or the couple may adjourn mediation to go into counselling. But there seems no reason why lawyer mediators shouldn't work more closely with counsellors, following collaborative practice. This is something that Resolution mediators may want to explore.

The traditional legal process offers its own kind of excellence. That is, an excellent legal and procedural framework that allows both sides to express their competing views by using excellent lawyers and that ensures that issues are considered in detail and fully probed. Resolution is achieved either in a negotiated settlement, usually conducted between lawyers, or in the finding of a judge who will have carefully listened to and analysed the facts and the different views put forward.

I certainly don't believe that any guidelines for identifying excellence should exclude those who provide it within the traditional process of ordinary representation.

But the adversarial system is inherently just that: adversarial, and as we know, it doesn't create the best conditions for couples working out their own best solutions for themselves and their families. It's in the nature of the process that legal principles and precedent tend to dominate over wider family interests and emotional considerations.

One of the big advantages of mediation and collaborative family law is that these actually provide within their systemic framework for wider issues to be taken into account than the narrower legal issues that tend to dominate the traditional process. But in order to be effective, it is vital for the practitioners to be skilled in what they do, and have the wider knowledge, understandings and sensitivities that the processes envisage.

This in turn demands specialised skills training and a wider knowledge base than they might have expected in the traditional process. I was for some years an external examiner in family law at the College of Law and I was surprised that students learning family law were given no insights whatsoever into these issues, even on an introductory basis. Understandably, the College's concern was that there was so much black letter law and procedure to cover, there simply wasn't the time to include extraneous matter.

The trouble is that there is no follow-up after solicitors qualify and are able to start their family law practices. Resolution has done a great deal to overcome this shortcoming, but there are still lawyers whose concern remains with black letter law and who take the view that 'dealing with emotions is not part of my function'. Personally, I don't understand how any family lawyer can have that belief; but whatever the beliefs may be in traditional practice, mediators and collaborative practitioners simply couldn't and wouldn't function in that way.

That's why mediators and collaborative law practitioners have intensive skills training and why Resolution's ADR section has a conference such as this, with workshops and sessions on a range of relevant matters.

There is so much to learn about people and relationships and their behaviour that can be helpful to practitioners. Personally, I have never found it a chore, as it is all so fascinating. The more that I've looked into psychology and behaviour, the dynamics of relationship breakdown, systems and patterns, the more I want to know.

Years ago I was a member of a small group of family lawyers and mental health professionals, all of whom were also mediators, who got together under the name of The Family Transitions Group. We met periodically to explore ways of collaborating effectively on an inter-disciplinary basis. We explored different ways of working, including for example having a counsellor present in a mediation session, and therapists liaising with the parties' lawyers, with the parties' specific consent of course. We shared our knowledge and our different perspectives, and tested other ways of cooperating on an inter-disciplinary basis, both within the group and outside of it. I remember for example my opposite number and I meeting with a child's therapist to discuss the best interests of a child in the context of a very difficult potential application to remove a child from the jurisdiction. That single session actually led shortly afterwards to a resolution of the dispute.

I'm sure that there is a lot more scope like that initiative for developing inter-disciplinary work, which would benefit the public and the professions.

And my final proposition . . .

Proposition No. 6: Balance is crucial

As one of my teaching resources, I've created a mediation construct, which is a pyramid with a base of four building blocks, each containing a fundamental mediation element, with three blocks on the next level up, two on the next, and a single block at the top. This element poised at the top is, appropriately called *balance*.

In mediation, balance between the parties, even-handedness and impartiality are of course inherent in the process. But there are many other balances that need to be struck in working effectively in mediation and collaborative law.

I want to touch on two of the areas of balance. One is the balance between rights and interests, and the other is the balance between the individual and the family. And to some extent, these aspects are of course inter-related.

Ideally, people whose marriage has broken down will find a delicate balance between their respective legal rights, so far as they can assess what those are, and their interests; and also a balance between their own personal interests and those of their family as a whole. But when people are going through the trauma of a marriage breakdown, they are not always minded to act ideally.

This is where both mediation and collaborative law can help, by helping people beyond their instinctive reactions and into looking more broadly at the family as a whole. As I see it, each of the couple should make their individual decisions on a fully informed basis, which includes having a complete financial picture and having the best possible assessment of what their legal rights and entitlement might be. This applies equally in mediation or collaborative law. But financial data and legal rights are obviously not the only criteria for decision-making and as we know, there are better ways to negotiate than pure positional bargaining.

But in any model of negotiation, parties are reassured by having their lawyers available in the process, which is a key premise of collaborative practice. This is one of the reasons why I've previously expressed a view about the need for the parties' lawyers to have a greater involvement in the mediation process in appropriate cases. This doesn't mean having lawyers attend every mediation, or every session, which would change the dynamic, but rather that lawyers should be able to engage more directly with the mediator, and that they should have a greater role in financial disclosure and in advising their clients as the mediation develops. They should also be able to attend some sessions, especially if their client feels the need for that support or if the couple are getting conflicting legal advice, which is affecting progress. With the benefit of hindsight, I think that the process we devised didn't give the lawyers an adequate role, while nevertheless leaving them with responsibility for the outcome reached without their involvement.

This aspect needs further consideration, especially as it has funding implications both for private clients and for public funding. There may need to be clearer criteria as to when a lawyer should be more closely involved in the process; but I wonder whether the fact that mediation hasn't become more widespread in privately funded cases may not have something to do with the concerns of both clients and lawyers about the substantial exclusion of lawyers from the process.

Mediators and collaborative practitioners are able to help people establish balance in their negotiations and find an agreed solution that works for both individuals and for the family as a whole, which minimises conflict and hostility, and which saves costs. Ultimately it is the parties' call as to how they respond to that guidance.

Conclusion

This concludes the six propositions, which indicate that while excellence can exist in the traditional legal process, it's likely to be more rewarding for the parties and the practitioners in mediation or collaborative practice, with their wider perspective and greater opportunities for humanity and healing.

They also suggest that more work remains to be done in developing and cross-pollenating models of practice and in exploring guidelines for the legal profession and for others including mental health professionals as to what currently constitutes good practice in the use of different processes and options in family breakdown. Without rigidifying, of course.

Inter-disciplinary cooperation has developed enormously over the last decade or so, and clearly there is scope to explore how this can be taken even further.

Lawyers have not always had a good press, and often get the blame for exacerbating difficult situations. Sometimes this is justified, but commonly it's the client who is pressing them to act aggressively while they are trying to help the client to adopt a more reasonable approach. In fact, lawyers have been in the forefront of moves to find better and less conflictual ways of helping couples to resolve their issues, and I think that without becoming complacent, we can have some pride in our contributions to the development of all-issues mediation and collaborative practice.

In conclusion, I'd like to turn, appropriately enough, to South Africa for a final word on legal practice. The Nelson Mandela School of Law (the Faculty of Law) at Fort Hare University in South Africa includes the following in the expression of its values, 'The management, staff and students of the School of Law will strive to be consistently guided by the values of humanity, egalitarianism, non-racialism, societal leadership, and excellence.' Now isn't that a nice way of expressing excellence in law?

Index